The Church as the Kingdom

It is quite possible that, if enough people in the Church read these pages and take them to heart, this book could inaugurate a new era in the life of the Church. The question is can we face belonging to a Church which is more vulnerable and more demanding but in the end more full of Christ's hope than Western Christians have grown accustomed to?

There is here a touch of real prophecy, which discerns the times and chooses it moment.

The Archdeacon of Rochester
The Venerable Michael Turnbull

I am excited that an Anglican parish priest is writing about the renewal of the church in Britain from the grassroots up, and doing so in terms which are essentially practical and relevant to our own situation. To date, too few books like this one have come out of the UK. We have been too dependent on imported books. This book is one that will most certainly help to rectify the balance.

It is readable too!

Jeanne Hinton
Writer and communicator, formerly
Editor *GrassRoots Magazine* (now *Christian*).

*To Dee, David, Patrick, Neil
and John-Daniel*

Cover photograph by Nigel Hearden

The Church as the Kingdom

A New Way of Being the Church

Peter Price

Marshall Pickering

Marshall Morgan and Scott
Marshall Pickering
3 Beggarwood Lane, Basingstoke, Hants RG23 7LP, UK

Copyright © 1987 by Peter Price
First published in 1987 by Marshall Morgan and Scott
Publications Ltd
Part of the Marshall Pickering Holdings Group
A subsidiary of the Zondervan Corporation

British Library CIP Data

Price, Peter
  The church as the kingdom.
  1. Church
  I. Title
260   BV600.2

ISBN 0–551–01426–1

Text Phototypeset in Linotron Times 10 on 11 point
by Input Typesetting Ltd, London SW19 8DR
Printed in Great Britain by
Guernsey Press Ltd, Guernsey C.I.

Contents

Foreword

A wise friend recently challenged the four bishops who work in the Anglican Diocese of Southwark (a Diocesan bishop and three suffragans) to spend more time thinking about the Church of the future. He observed that we spent almost all our time responding to the clamourous demands of the present, and in this sense 'keeping things going'. Was it not important, he said, to ask ourselves what kind of a church we thought the diocese ought to be, and what values it ought to reflect into the community at large? How else could we know what to strengthen and what to give up, and what kind of vision to share with all our fellow christians in the common task?

It has been a struggle to make time to do what he suggested. But we are beginning. And I find that many of the things we are saying to each other about the future of the church are precisely the points which Peter Price has raised in this stimulating book. He argues once again, as others have done before him, that the church is not an end in itself; it exists to make known the loving rule or Kingdom of God, and to help others find meaning and hope for their life through its witness. The author has drawn on the experience of the church outside Britain to help us understand what it means to belong to a 'Basic Christian Community', and uses this concept to break down some of the tired and ineffective theology which still rules so much of church life today.

I am very grateful to the author, a priest in this diocese, for making me think so positively and hard about words I often use too easily, like 'mission' and 'Kingdom'. I believe this is a timely book, of the kind which draws together a number of different strands in contemporary church life and thought, and then focuses them in a fresh and comprehensive way. Above all it is a hopeful book, rooted in biblical faith, and therefore disturbing and encouraging at the same time.

Ronald Bowlby
Bishop of Southwark
January 1987

Preface

This book is about a new way of being the Church. It is about Christian communities. Of course as the writer of Ecclesiastes reminds us 'There is nothing new under the sun', and Christian communities are not new as structures by which the Church has sought to regain its vision for mission. Monastic orders, Franciscans, the Little Brothers and Sisters of Jesus, Taize, Lee Abbey, Corrymeela, the Community of Celebration are among countless communities who have sought to re-adjust the compass of the Church in its life and witness. The communities of the people, neighbourhood or basic communities are a new way of being the Church.

This book had its beginnings among the Community of Celebration on the Isle of Cumbrae in the Clyde estuary. It was here that I stayed while trying to make sense of some bits of my life and my sense of failure about community living. I picked up a copy of *Sojourners*, the magazine of an inner city Christian community in Washington DC. I read about evangelical charismatic christians who were getting their hands dirty with the concerns of Christ for the poor, the hungry and those oppressed by violence or the fear of the ultimate violence of nuclear war. Here I learned of people living in cummunities among the poor. I was discovering the experience of Latin American Christians and others who demonstrated a new way of being the Church.

While preparing a paper for a course at St George's House

Windsor, I began to look at ways in which the experience of communities and what have become known as Basic Christian Communities have relevance to the institutional Church in the West and in particular to the United Kingdom. This book is an expansion of that thinking.

In reflecting on the impending cataclysm that threatens to engulf our nation, with its growing social disintegration and violence, I began to hope for a Church that would have compassion at its heart, a new vitality in sharing Jesus Christ, a willingness to become poorer and go beyond the immediate resources to express a truer love for human beings who are so precious to God.

The biggest factor in all this is *will*. Is there among the Christian people of the West the will to see things changed? Do we have sufficient compassion for the poor, the outcast, the lonely, the stranger and the fearful? Do we desire a change in our society that gives us some of the hallmarks of the Kingdom of God in a way that is visible? Do we have a hope for our world to live without fear of nuclear annihilation? It is something of this struggle with the will that this book seeks to engage. It's not an answer book. It is a book of pointers. It is not a how-to-do-it book; that I hope will follow. It is a book born out of a desire for the timelessness of the Kingdom of God in the Gospel of Jesus Christ to be shared and lived among ordinary people, by ordinary people who can build an extraordinary way of being.

I write as an anglican, a member of the Church of England, a vicar of a suburban parish. I have endeavoured to reflect ecumenically about the Church. Of course particular illustrations from my own history will reflect my own story, but in the writing of this book I am grateful to people of all Christian traditions and none. Many have expressed a hope that with sufficient will there may be just enough time to save this generation. I hope so. This is written in that hope because in Christ we have been called to 'a living hope'. Living that hope means believing that change can and will happen.

So many people have influenced and helped me in my thinking, and several are mentioned in this book. My deepest appreciation is for my wife Dee. She has been a constant source of inspiration, wisdom and encouragement – and at the moments of self soubt has believed in me and the task. I am grateful to our many friends who have shared and challenged our thinking, particularly Dr. Wyn Williams, Deaconess Sylvia Roberts and canon Roy White. Thanks are due to Debbie Thorpe of Marshall Pickering for encouraging me to write the book, and to Val Nobbs for her helpful and senstive editing of the manuscript. I owe a debt of gratitude to Shauna Brown for typing the text, and to Ursula Owen for reading and completing work on it and finally to Sister Deirdre of the Emmaus Retreat Centre at West Wickham for solitude and hospitality.

Chapter One

A Relevant Church?

There is a hunger for meaning and relevance to life, among many people in the West. It is a searching, all-consuming hunger. It touches the old and the young, the poor and the rich, the well-fed and the starving. It is a hunger that longs to be fed with meaning. Who are we? What are we here for? Where are we going? It is a hunger that looks at the institutions that appear to give relevance: the state, religion, education, business, the economy, and finds them wanting.

Many people find it hard to make sense of the misery of the world – its hunger, poverty, torture, death. They can make some sense of poverty when they see Mother Theresa; terminal illness and death can be faced with dignity, given the insights and care of Cicely Saunders and the Hospice movement. The evils of racial discrimination are exposed by Desmond Tutu, and even diplomacy is given some point by Terry Waite's combination of integrity and mediating skill. The imprisonment and torture of Sheila Cassidy in a Chilean gaol – her crime, the giving of medical help to a terrorist – are given some meaning by the faith she re-discovered there.

Most people in the UK make little sense of the Church. It does not appear to be relevant. It seems to address questions no one is asking and when it does comment on contemporary issues it seems naive and confused. When Church leaders speak publicly about faith, it seems more like doubt, and the subject matter of the virgin birth and the resurrection are beyond the daily conversation of most people. To women it appears sexist; to the non-academic it is elitist; to the working man it is classist, and by its denominationalism it disrupts people's ability to see God. To those with the simplest knowledge of its founder, Jesus Christ, the Church seems a far cry from the egalitarian community which it claims inspires its life.

For most ordinary people life is given shape by food, shelter, clothing, security, health, and for many, justice and freedom from oppression. Most people take these things for granted, believing them to be available to all. When these things are lacking people feel crushed. Some believe it is appropriate for the Church to do something, to commit itself to social action for the homeless, the poor, the handicapped or those facing other deprivation. When it so acts people can see it to be relevant.

Making sense of things

Other people feel the Church should not be concerned with making sense of things in the here and now but with preparing people for the life to come. But the Christian message does concern itself with giving meaning to the present. It also concerns itself with the future, a future that will make sense of things that are impossible to understand here and now. The danger for the Church in its search for relevance is that it often substitutes human idealism for Christian hope. Christians are in danger of opting for a false utopia by yielding to the temptation to be relevant in the wrong ways.

The first temptation faced by Jesus in the wilderness was to turn stones into bread, and by providing resources to feed the hungry be seen to be relevant. If he could do that he could become a one-man 'Band Aid' and surely all the world would believe! But Jesus knew that simply providing for material needs does not change human life. His calling is to identify and suffer with humankind. Jesus highlights the tension that exists between meeting people's needs and enabling them to discover what God intended them to be – in harmony with himself and with each other. Jesus did feed the hungry – it was integral to his message. Witness the mass feedings of four and five thousand people at a time and his declared policy in his 'sheep and goats' speech where the citizens of the kingdom of God will have fed the hungry, clothed the naked, visited the imprisoned and given shelter to the stranger. But to this manifesto Jesus adds that he will be recognised in the world among those who are on the margins of society and his love will be shown through care and compassion.

Today we live in a world rich in natural resources – oil, coal, minerals, food distributed throughout the world. Yet their blatant misuse is revealed in energy shortages, famines and the growth of deserts. The African famine of 1984/85 provides us with a stark example. The arms trade, nuclear arsenals and the global militarisation connived at by both East and West create delusions of security and control, of power and powerlessness.

Affluence and poverty

In a recent survey of Christian wealth it has been estimated that 'Jesus today has 1.5 billion followers whose annual income in US dollars is 6.5 trillion and these followers own two-thirds of the world's entire resources!'[1] Such a statistic raises the question 'what is the relevance of a Church that is overwhelmingly the Church of the rich?' Its wealth has created demands for security in order to maintain standards of affluence, health and shelter in which most of its members live. The Church of the rich is a Church that depends for its security upon military defence. Expenditure on arms increased from 236 billion dollars in 1969 to 650 billion dollars by 1982. The superpowers have accounted for fifty-three per cent of these sums. By 1985 the USSR was expected to spend 300 billion dollars per year, while from 1982 the USA had a five year programme estimated at two trillion dollars. To put a human perspective on such astronomic sums, they amount to 140 dollars per head for every man, woman and child on the planet.

In the West, Christian people are heavily dependent upon the arms race for their livelihood. Worldwide some 100 million people are employed in defence related jobs. About sixty million of these are Christians – government leaders, employees, employers, scientists and technicians, as well as clerks and typists.

This expenditure represents a mass squandering of resources, physical, material and human. Many Christians are deeply concerned about the implications of such expenditure. Their concern gives momentum to these questions – Who is God for us? Whom do we serve? In whom do we place our security?

Many millions among the world's poor have a different view of life. The World Bank report of 1980 described absolute poverty as 'a condition of life so characterised by malnutrition and disease as to be beneath any reasonable definition of human decency'.[2] In 1983, 800 million people were deemed to be living in absolute poverty. This figure represents one third of the Third World population, but just as disturbing is that hidden in this statistic are millions of our fellow Christians. Other statistics highlight the problem another way: 750 million affluent and comparatively comfortable Christians are willing to let 195 million brothers and sisters in Christ live in absolute poverty.

In the West, we think of poverty and wealth as primarily matters of material concern. In the poor Church, poverty and wealth are measured differently: the Church of the West is spiritually poor; the materially poor Church is spiritually rich. The lifestyle of the rich Church parallels that of the secular world in which it is set; the lifestyle of the poor Church parallels the simplicity of Jesus and the community of the early Church. The poor Church is a sign of hope for the rich Church, if we have ears to hear and eyes to see. The poor Church is a community Church, the experience of 200,000 base ecclesial communities in Latin America bearing testimony to this. It is a Church of the lowest social groupings, as shown by the thirty million strong African indigenous Churches; it is a Spirit-filled and evangelistic Church, as evidenced by the 5.5 million charismatic Christians of India and Asia. The 1985 Statistical Table on Global Mission[3] reveals that China has a house Church movement of ninety-eight million and that some 250 million people in China are aware of Christianity, Christ and the Gospel.

Rich church – poor church

The spiritual wealth of the Church of the poor demonstrates a gospel that is being heard as good news to people in the situation in which they are living. It is a gospel that exposes the faithfulness of the manifesto of Jesus (Luke 4:18–19), it is 'good news to the poor . . . release to the captives . . . recovering of sight to the blind . . . liberty to those who are oppressed'. It is a gospel that has ushered in the 'acceptable year of the Lord'; this is shown in new relationships, forgiveness of enemies and oppressors, a sharing of goods, a caring for the whole family of God's people – especially the most needy. It is a gospel that makes the Church relevant because it meets people in the 'here and now', answering their questions, and pointing to the future coming of the kingdom on earth as it is in heaven.

The spiritual wealth of the Church of the poor exposes the naked spiritual poverty of the Church of the West. The Church of the rich has nothing relevant to say to the world, except as a warning against the dangers of affluence, supporting the status quo and its separation of faith and life. Its affluence and involvement in the arms race make it a party to oppression. Although its members in the USA earn more than fourteen times what its members earn in India, the amount of wealth it gives away is minimal. The poor remain poor, because the rich remain rich. The West has ignored the warning of God in 1 John: 'If anyone has this world's goods and sees his brother in need, yet closes his heart against him . . . how does God's love abide in him? . . . Little children let us not love in word and speech but in deed and in truth . . .' What poor Christians fear are the consequences of the self-interest of rich Christians. As recently as 1983 this was expressed at Vancouver at the World Council of Churches Sixth General Assembly: 'The North Atlantic Churches agenda was dominated by the question of peace and nuclear war, while that of the rest of the Churches had to do with hunger, poverty and political oppression'.[4] The North Atlantic Churches, in spite of much discussion, held the upper hand at the Congress. Poor Christians see rich Christians becoming sensitive to the issue of defence but what they fear is that even if arms reduction becomes a reality it will only mean greater affluence for the West and continued oppression of the poor.

For centuries the Christian Church in the West has been in a place of privilege. In England, being English is, more often than not, seen as being synonymous with being Christian. Our Churches do not call into question the control by governments of security, law and order or economics, despite many blatant examples of injustice, oppression and illegality. Our Churches do not ask just who decides who our 'enemies' are. We forget, or rationalise, the command of Jesus that we 'love our enemies'.

'Christians', writes Lesslie Newbiggin, 'are not distinguishable as people who obviously live by different commitments from their neighbours. And I should doubt whether it is normal on the other side of the water to find that Christians are regarded as centres of "un-American" activities'.[5] This lack of distinction contributes to the irrelevance of the Church in the eyes of most people.

The problem for the Church in the UK is that it is expected to guard and sustain the culture of which it is a part. Hence a Conservative Member of Parliament, in response to the Archbishop of Canterbury's challenge to do something about poverty in the inner cities, could say, 'This is not the Christianity we were brought up to believe in.' By and large the Church has not seen itself bearing God's judgement to the society in which it is set. Neither can it, for it has been reduced to 'a good cause', and its gospel a spiritual aspirin. The values which society allows it to promote are essentially personal. Once the Church challenges underlying causes of injustice, poverty and disorder, it is condemned for being political and declared out of order. The question as to whether the gospel is anything more than a spiritual pain reliever, helping people know a Jesus who alleviates our anxiety and guilt, is never raised.

The poor Church does speak of judgement, regardless of the consequences. Addressing the Eloff Inquiry into the South African Council of Churches, Bishop Desmond Tutu spoke in the context of Scripture – 'God's purposes are certain. They may remove a Tutu; they may remove the South African Council of Churches, but God's intention to establish his Kingdom of justice, of love, of compassion, will not be thwarted. We are not scared, certainly not of the Government, or any of the other perpetrators of injustice and oppression, for victory is ours through him who loved us. . . Apartheid is as evil and vicious as Nazism and Communism, and the Government will fail completely for ranging itself on the side of evil, injustice and oppression. The Government is not God, they are just ordinary human beings who very soon like other tyrants before them will bite the dust.'[6]

There are signs of hope in the Western Church. At a meeting of top military leaders in the USA recently, the statement was made, 'The greatest challenge to all we do now comes from within the Churches.'[7] This was a reflection not only on the growing opposition to nuclear arms, but the growing disobedience of the Churches over government policy on refugees from tyranny in Central America. 'National Church bodies are now seriously discussing the theological basis and spiritual imperative for civil disobedience. Issues such as war tax resistance, prayerful trespass at nuclear facilities, sanctuary, non-violent resistance over Central America and South Africa and non-registration for the draft are all pressing issues in many Churches.'[8]

Challenging and relevant

The Church has to be seen to be 'challengingly relevant'.[9] Such a Church will face opposition which in the West is comparatively benign at present, and non-existent in the UK where the Church is not a threat to established structures. The poor Church has long been used to a litany of suffering, torture, imprisonment and death. A Church that faces its role as witness will have to count the cost of its suffering. The Church must proclaim a gospel which makes people face questions they have never precisely faced. The questions are fundamental – 'Who is God for us?' 'In whom do we place our security?' 'Whom do we serve?' Facing into them will expose inconsistencies of Christian living and lifestyle and we shall have to change. Christian experience is about change, repentance, new life and hope. To achieve that new life there has to be judgement, death and the power of grace and love, among and for God's people the Church.

What about the Church in the UK? How is it to be challengingly relevant? At present it is a Church bedevilled by compromise and conformity. Even the most non-conformist groups reveal deep conformity to the world around them. It is a Church that places great emphasis on the individual. In its more fundamentalist forms it stresses the need to be personally convicted of sin. In its more established forms personal sin and guilt are heavily emphasised, together with confession and absolution. Most preachers appeal for a personal or individual response to their message. Few Churches encourage their members as a body to repent of corporate involvement in sin; sins expressed in prejudice, complicity with the arms race, failure to respond to the needs of the hungry and the oppressed, and those in prison for conscience sake. Even fewer Churches encourage their leaders to speak out in judgement where the law of God is being violated. Little is done, as a body, to radically evaluate lifestyle.

Individualism in Christianity creates schizophrenia. People live in two different spheres by two different standards. They live in the world; and they live in the Church. At work most have to conform to the prevailing standards applied within the company or organisation. Personal ethics, questions of right and wrong relate only to such matters as whether a person steals time or property from the institution. Bigger questions of justice and fair play simply become submerged, because the greater good of the organisation for which people work is at stake.

Questions about right and wrong have been relegated to the place of personal judgement, and how we behave at home. In the work situation, most Christian people are aware of the choices that have to be made. The choice is between suffering and compromise. The fact that most people choose compromise is not surprising. Christianity has been reduced to an individual response to God and society. There is insufficient solidarity or fellowship to enable people to bear the suffering involved in losing a job, a home, status or privilege for the sake of Jesus Christ. Like the rich young man Christians are faced with the problem of knowing the commitment, but simply having too much to lose.

The task of the Holy Spirit is 'to convict the world of sin, of righteousness (justice) and judgement' (John 16:8). Such a task cannot be interpreted purely at the level of individual conversion. It has to be a task which tackles the structure of society in the places where human beings are denied their full humanity. The gospel is concerned with economic justice; political feedom; the breaking down of barriers of culture, race, sex, ecology; as well as in offering hope, drawing people out of a sense of apathy and hopelessness about their condition.

The witness of the poor Church is powerful precisely because, in the midst of suffering, it has found hope. It is convicting the societies in which it is set by challenging struc-

tures that are unjust and oppressive. In many places this judgement of society has brought about conviction of sin, and made
a stepping stone to justice.

To be challengingly relevant the Church in the West, needs
to re-evaluate the fundamental mission of Jesus. The bottom
line is to recognise that Jesus did not come to found a Church,
but to reveal a Kingdom. If the Church in the West is to have
relevance to God's purpose it has to rediscover the mission of
Jesus in announcing God's Kingdom. The Church has to realise
it is not an end in itself; it is a sign of the Kingdom of God, and
its members are, first and foremost, citizens of that Kingdom.

Notes

1. Survey of Christian Financial Resources 1980: 'Silver and gold have I none', David Barrett: *International Bulletin of Missionary Research* October 1983. All additional statistics in this chapter unless otherwise stated come from this report.
2. International Bank for Reconstruction and Development: *World Development Report* (Washington DC World Bank HQ), p. 32.
3. *Annual Statistical Table on Global Mission 1985*, David Barrett: IBMR.
4. *Constructing Local Theologies*, Robert J. Schreiter: SCM, 1985, p. 3.
5. 'Mission in the 1980's': Lesslie Newbiggin: *Occasional Bulletin for Mission Research*, October 1980.
6. *Hope and Suffering*, Desmond Tutu: Fount, pp. 138, 158.
7. *Sojourners*, April 1985.
8. *The Rise of Christian Conscience*, Jim Wallis, January 1985.
9. Lesslie Newbiggin, *op cit*.

Chapter Two

A Kingdom People

The Kingdom of God is a society into which Jesus invites people. The society is marked by those who recognise that the values, lifestyle and rulers of this world do not fulfil the purpose of God. To enter, the Kingdom demands a response, a willingness to change, to turn away from previously held attitudes, behaviour and lifestyle; to submit to repentance. The Greek word for repentance is 'metanoia' and it carries within it the idea of both turning and the process of change. The root of the word is 'meta', the same root as 'metamorphosis'. Metamorphosis is the process by which a caterpillar changes into a butterfly. The idea of repentance is that it is ongoing, changing the attitudes at the heart of our being, and transforming the person into the likeness of the king, Jesus Christ. Repentance is the way in by which people are invited to enter; and the Kingdom is formed as those people together submit their lives to the process of change.

This Kingdom Jesus brought is good news that is to be believed. It is of such a quality that it will not be found inadequate, and it is worth staking all to obtain membership (Matthew 14:44–45). It is good news for poor, captive, blind and oppressed people (Mark 1:14–16; Luke 4:18–19). It is good news because it offers hope, liberty, sight and freedom to such people. It is a Kingdom that is for 'here and now' as well as 'there and then'. It is a Kingdom whose liberating power is expressed both in physical and spiritual terms and it cannot be proclaimed effectively by emphasising one aspect without the other.

In the development of Jesus' message of liberation, often called the sermon on the mount (Matthew 5:1–12; Luke 6:17 and 20–22) both the physical and spiritual aspects of the Kingdom are balanced. Matthew's gospel emphasises the spiritual dimension while Luke develops the physical. Jesus is accredited in Matthew, for example, as saying 'Blessed are the poor in spirit, for theirs is the kingdom of heaven' while Luke records Jesus as saying 'Blessed are you poor, for yours is the kingdom of God'. To be poor is also to be poor in spirit. Much Christian thinking and behaviour has gone wrong when one aspect, rather than both aspects, have been emphasised in teaching and lifestyle.

The Kingdom of God, into which Jesus invites people, is a Kingdom of the spirit. It is a Kingdom whose citizens are to pray that it shall be seen 'on earth, as it is in heaven' (Matthew 6:10). It cannot simply be regarded as future, and it is not the creation of human beings. It is a Kingdom 'whose maker and builder is God' (Hebrews 10:8). This Kingdom has no court favourites, although the king clearly has a bias towards the poor (Matthew 22: 1–10), a bias that should be reflected in the lives and intentions of its citizens. The concerns of the king are of one who, looking at the struggles of humanity, anxious for food, security and safety, calls for the kind of justice and peace in relationships where such anxieties can cease. The way that God governs the Kingdom is to share its government, first by putting it into the hands of Jesus (Luke 12:30–32) who in turn will put it into the hands of its citizens (Luke 22:28–30).

Rulers of kingdoms demand loyalty and allegiance; in return they offer privilege and status. The Kingdom of God offers status and privilege by making its citizens 'inheritors of the kingdom' or 'children of God'. The demands of God's Kingdom transcend all other personal, moral, political and societal claims for allegiance. The rule of God is not to be compromised and to obey it is to make a choice between 'God and mammon'

(Matthew 6:24). 'Mammon' is usually associated with money but it has to do with all the sources of security and power that take away from God his right to rule.

The kingdom of God is the radical alternative to all other kingdoms and rulers. To give allegiance to it calls for a continual re-evaluation of our values, attitudes, behaviour and thinking.

A political Kingdom

The Kingdom of God is political. In Christmas carol services a passage from Isaiah which refers to the political status of Jesus is often quoted. Its significance is lost on us today. 'For to us a child is born, to us a son is given, and the government will be upon his shoulder . . . of the increase of his government and of peace there will be no end; upon the throne of David, and over his kingdom to establish it, and to uphold it with justice and righteousness from this time forth and for evermore' (Isaiah 9:6–7). The rule of God is about the things that matter to humankind. The citizens of the Kingdom of God are to share in the establishing of a Kingdom of peace, justice and righteousness. This will take our activity as God's people right to the heart of the struggle for liberation.

For many people to describe the Kingdom of God as 'political' will be disturbing. Politics has to do with being governed, and it is in this sense that the word 'political' is used to describe the Kingdom of God. Jesus fed the hungry, mixed with social outcasts, challenged the powerful and revealed himself as Messiah to a woman. He identified the Kingdom of God with the basic struggles of humanity against political oppression; cultural, racist and sexist alienation; the destruction of the environment through industrialisation and exploitation. This political Kingdom is personal too. It has been described as 'the struggle for assurance against apathy in personal life'.[1] This struggle is reflected in Jesus' intention that the Kingdom should provide 'life in all its fullness'. (John 10:10).

The atmosphere in which Jesus was nurtured and in which he lived his life was one in which politics and religion were inextricably intertwined. He was born into a nation under occupation, a nation aching for deliverance. People constantly looked for signs of a Messiah, a Deliverer, the expectation of whom had been integral to Jewish teaching and hope for generations. As the child Jesus was initiated into Jewish faith and practice, days after his birth, the expectation of being a Deliverer was laid on him. The prophetess Anna 'spoke of him to all who were looking for the redemption of Israel' (Luke 2:38). Simeon, the priest, recognised in Jesus the long-awaited Messiah. Zechariah, the father of John the Baptist, spoke of God as 'visiting and redeeming his people . . .' in such a way that they 'should be saved from their enemies' and having received that deliverance 'might serve him (God) without fear' (Luke 1: 71–74). To these people enemies were flesh and blood, and deliverance from them was expected in similar terms.

Jesus' command to 'love your enemies' was spoken in the context of the Roman occupation. Jesus knew how hard it was to love people who even he saw as a threat to the future of Jerusalem (Luke 19:43). As he taught, he could see the 'eagles', the standards of the Romans, gathering around the remains of Israel (Luke 17:37). He warned his hearers to read the signs of the times, he commanded them to change (Luke 13:3 and 5) and to pray for those who hated and persecuted them (Luke 6:27–28).

Jesus' assessment of the enemies his fellow countrymen faced was realistic, as was his assessment of rulers and governments. His call to conversion and repentance, however, was not directed in the first instance at the enemy, 'the pagans', but at the people who claimed to have faith. He saw them as needing to undergo inward change through repentance, renewed attitudes and lifestyle. Such changes would be positive acts of resistance towards the enemy, leading to the possibility of reconciliation (Luke 6:27–28).

Jesus warned that if people did not read the signs of the

times and strive to make peace with enemies and accusers, they would invite inevitable destruction. The radical command to 'love enemies' and pray for those who persecute and do all manner of evil, was to give to the Kingdom a cutting edge with which few could reckon.

To 'love our enemies' pre-supposes that we have such. In trying to make sense of Jesus' teaching in the light of the dominance of security and defence in our national life, the Church has to ask the question 'Who decides who our enemies are?' Our nation is often described as 'Christian'. This is a misrepresentation, but it somehow leads people to the view that there is something intrinsically more Christian about capitalism than Fascism or Communism. The Church has all too easily been beguiled into letting the state mould our opinions as to who our enemies are and what our standard of living should be – a standard of living that oppresses the poor and encourages racial, cultural and sexual discrimination.

Jesus told his disciples that the rulers of the world establish and keep their power by lording it over their subjects. He understood the nature of rulers, well, he was not in the least naive. He saw that rulers once established, then presume to describe themselves as benefactors to those whom they have made their subjects (Luke 22:24–27)!

Jesus used this illustration to show that the rule of God does not operate this way. It is a rule marked by service and example. If necessary that example takes self-sacrifice to the point of death itself. The servants of the king are elevated to the status of friends. The pattern of rule is set by the words, 'Greater love has no man than this, that a man lay down his life for his friends. You are my friends if you do what I command you . . . This I command you, to love one another' (John 15:13–14 and 17). To submit to the rule of this Kingdom is first to receive love, and having received love, to give it without qualification.

A Kingdom of power

Jesus shares with his disciples the way that power is to be practised in the Kingdom of God: 'I am among you as one who serves' (Luke 22:27). Status, formerly the preserve of the eldest in the community, is just as valid for the youngest. Leaders are marked not by the way others serve them, but in the way they serve others. There is not the least bit of irony in Jesus' description of himself as 'servant'. He is not like the civil servant whose task is to keep people in submission to the laws of the state. He is a servant because he does the menial things; accepts the abuse of others; allows himself to bear their griefs and pains; even accepts accusation and blame from others for things that he has never done. Such laws and practices turn upside down the priorities of the world.

Where it is practised Kingdom lifestyle produces opposition. Jesus recognised that such a rule would bring a reaction, often in the shape of violence. 'I', he said, 'have not come to bring peace but a sword' (Matthew 10:34). While inheritance is promised to the citizens of the Kingdom, it is for those who have continued in the struggle . . . 'who have continued with me in my trials . . .' (Luke 22:28). It is with those who are struggling that Jesus is identified. His place is among the lowest and the poor (Philippians 2:8). His power is not made effective by frightening people, nor by associating with the high and mighty. Jesus does not threaten those who are 'least' in the world; the little ones, the frightened and oppressed. Jesus reveals God's desire for justice among those who are poor, oppressed and marginalised. His life and his death are to set people free: they are a declaration that God has set himself the task of 'hanging in' with the struggle until his Kingdom comes on earth as it is in heaven.

It is to this Kingdom that the Church has to pay close attention. To be challengingly relevant, the Church in the West, and particularly in the UK, has to take to heart its role as a sign of the kingdom of God. To be a sign, the Church has to understand God's presence and activity in history. Jesus perceived God's presence and activity in history, and it was within flesh and blood encounters and relationships that Jesus endeavoured to do his Father's work. Jesus met and dealt with things as they were. Events were not manipulated in order that God's purpose could be fulfilled. Jesus, as a man in his time, was also of his time, and yet out of his time. Paradoxically God could achieve his purpose in, through, and in spite of human action. Jesus died on a cross, not because God willed it first and foremost, but because human response and reaction to the things that Jesus did and said, made his continuing freedom and life a threat to the status quo.

Jesus is the model for all who follow the rule of God. The prophecies of the Old Testament, particularly those of the suffering of a servant figure (Isaiah 52:13–53:12) were intended as a picture of what happens to any of God's people who strive to follow the law of love to its conclusion. Yet Jesus' life and death are mirrored in the picture of the suffering servant and this is significant. His life and death reflect the consequences of total self-giving and service to God's purpose in redeeming the world.

In recognising God's presence throughout history, the Church must participate in God's activity in the here and now. We have to read the signs of the times in the struggle of the poor for economic justice; the oppressed for political freedom; the alienated, culturally, racially and sexually in finding hope. At the root of the struggle lies a call for non-conformity to the standards, attitudes and prejudices around us: 'Do not be conformed to the world,' writes St Paul, 'but be transformed by the renewal of your mind, that you may prove what is the will of God, what is good, acceptable and perfect' (Romans 12:2). If the Church in the West is to be involved in this struggle it must undergo a process of conversion. This is an holistic conversion, seeing human beings delivered personally, economically, politically, culturally and ecologically. Such a conversion will no longer allow the concept of personal salvation simply to be the icing on the cake of already established and acceptable attitudes and lifestyle. Jesus' call to us is a call to repentance, that we may become a sign of the Kingdom.

A sign of the Kingdom

'This world is not a waiting room for the Kingdom of God . . . it is the battleground and construction site for the Kingdom which comes from God himself.'[2] To be a 'sign' of the Kingdom the Church must enter into the conflict and the building programme of the Kingdom of God. Jesus encouraged his disciples to 'read the signs of the times', in order to understand how God is present and to act in response to his presence. To many it will come as a surprise to discover that God is present in all situations, and that far from 'us' taking God into the world he has gone on ahead of us, and is waiting for us to catch up with him!

To read the signs of the times, we need to understand that human beings live and suffer on many different levels. People are complex, as is human experience. Reality is different for everybody and we need to grasp that in order to understand where God's Kingdom has to be seen at work. In the absence of the Church as an effective sign of the Kingdom, God is often disposed to use other signs – liberation groups, ethnic minority units, and peace protestors. This should challenge the Church to fulfil its ordained role in the world, to reveal the secret of the gospel 'so that the sovereignties and powers should learn only now, through the Church, how comprehensive God's wisdom really is' (Ephesians 3:10 JB).

Among the poor in many nations there is a struggle for economic justice. It is reflected in our own nation by what Lesslie Newbiggin has shown as contradictory principles operating against each other – 'a market economy based on the sovereignty of wants and a welfare system based on a sovereignty of needs. On each side the appeal is made to "rights" – the right of each person to enjoy what he has earned, and the right of each person to what is needed for a decent life . . .'[3] For the Church to enter into the struggle for economic justice it must recognise the reality of exploitation, and be willing to see the gospel as speaking to that situation, rather than simply reflecting one side or another of a political argument. The gospel of the Kingdom challenges the whole framework of economics, and its concern is that no one shall exploit or be exploited.

It is in the area of economic justice that Jesus found the greatest resistance in his own time. The Pharisees and Sadducees were middle class, affluent religious pietists. They had compromised with the occupying authority, the Romans, paying taxes in order to support their own lifestyle and piety unhindered. They had developed a system of rules which made them effectively untouchable by others of their own race. Tax collectors were regarded as unforgivable; and certain other social groupings including tanners, shepherds and women were unable to attain full acceptance by God. The system of sacrifice was based on the principle 'the more you pay the greater your standing in the eyes of God'. Hence the surprise of the disciples when the widow placed her two coins in the Temple treasury, and Jesus remarked, 'I tell you that this poor widow put more in the offering box than all the others. For the others put in what they had to spare of their riches; but she, poor as she is, put in all she had' (Mark 12:43, 44).

Compassion and love had been subjected to a system of rules and regulations, and when opportunities occurred for compassion to over-ride the fanaticism of a religion 'that made men right with God' fanaticism won. Jesus, on the other hand, was always looking for ways to show that compassion and love are God's way. He tells parable after parable, but in the story of the man who hired men at different hours throughout the day (Matthew 20:1–16) the point is made most strongly. Jesus knew what it was like to be without the means of earning food for the family. A denarius would provide wages for a family for only one day. To pay less was to totally disregard the value of the worker. With this story, and others like it, the whole economic system was brought into focus and the law of love and compassion turned on it. The fact that this story also reveals middle class exploitation of the poor should not be overlooked.

The poverty of the two-thirds world and the reality of economic injustice worldwide must challenge middle class Christians to a complete re-evaluation of the means by which we earn and the ways in which we use what we earn. It should lead us to look at the ways in which our own economic system exploits the needy and rewards the rich. Are we prepared to work for a more just economic system, even at cost to ourselves? In whom do we put our trust?

Amnesty International and other human rights groups draw attention to the struggle for human rights, another of the signs of the times. Human dignity is not high on the list of world priorities given the hunger, imprisonment, homelessness and inadequate health care that exist. Jesus recognised in his own people a desire for political freedom, but a desire which was motivated by revenge and hate. He recognised the futility of that route. He called in the first instance for a change of heart from his own people – not from their oppressors – and as servant himself, he set the example, 'Father forgive them . . . they know not what they do . . .'

The revolutionaries of Jesus' time – the Essenes, the Zealots – looked for a political freedom that would exalt the Jewish religion. Jesus rejected that route entirely, he was 'the light to lighten the Gentiles . . .' and the nearest Gentiles were the enemy oppressors, the Romans. The Kingdom of God cannot be identified as the exclusive possession of any culture, class, sex or nation.

The Church must see the presence of God in the struggle for human dignity amidst the famine of Africa, in the struggle for liberation in Central and Southern America, and in the townships of South Africa; but equally it must concern itself with those in the West who have been forced on to the margins of society by social, military and economic policies that leave them crying out for justice.

Solidarity – the mark of the Kingdom. Solidarity is not a biblical word, but it is a concept deeply rooted in the Bible. It is a word that means 'standing shoulder to shoulder, struggling together, suffering for one another and living with one another in a single community'.[4] It is a word used by Marxists in their language of class struggle; by blacks and Asians in their bid for racial equality; and by women's groups in their struggle for equal rights and liberation. It is a word of hope; a hope expressed by St. Paul, when he says 'There is neither Jew nor Greek, there is neither slave nor free, there is neither male nor female; for you are all one in Christ Jesus' (Galatians 3:28). Jesus challenged the incipient racism in his own society, the story of the Good Samaritan being one of the best examples of this challenge.

More radically, Jesus faced into a hornet's nest of prejudice and oppression in his attitude to women. Women were regarded as possessions, subject to the vagaries of men as either wives, chattels or prostitutes. Jesus' association with women was nothing short of scandalous and their companionship on his journeys around the country, where by his own admittance he frequently 'had nowhere to lay his head', caused many an eyebrow to be raised. The gospels use a number of devices to reveal for us the status given by Jesus to women, but perhaps the most startling is that revealed by the witnesses to the resurrection. Women were simply not allowed to give testimony in court; their witness was regarded by a patriarchal society as unreliable and perjurious. Yet, the most significant event in the history of the world, the resurrection of Jesus Christ from the dead, is evidenced by a woman!

It has taken feminist and women's liberation groups to make the Church face into the scandal of injustice and oppression faced by women in both its life and in society. In the area of women's ministry in the Anglican Church the oppression continues. As recently as April 1985, the 'Church Society' expressed the view that the ordination of women 'would reverse the created relationship of the sexes which the New Testament gives as the basis of Church order, and would therefore be contrary to the revealed will of God in Holy Scripture'.[5] This statement runs counter to that expressed by Rabbi Alexander Shapiro, President of the Rabbinical Assembly, the international governing body of Conservative Judaism, who recognising the ordination of women as Rabbis said, 'This represents a recognition that all of us, both men and women, are created in God's image and that the potential for spiritual greatness exists in all human beings.' Or less prosaically, as the first woman Rabbi of the Assembly, Amy Eilberg said – 'Jewish women need never again feel gender is a barrier to their full participation in Jewish life'.[6] Such a cry is expressed by women within and without the Church worldwide and is understood by Jesus.

It is in a spirit of repentance, and with a willingness to submit to a process of change that the Church in the UK must re-evaluate its life in the light of Jesus' mission to announce a Kingdom. Such a re-evaluation must take into account the spiritual wealth of the poor Church, and it is to this that we will now turn our attention.

Notes

1. *On Human Dignity*, Jurgen Moltmann: SCM, p. 110.
2. Moltmann, *op cit.*, p. 109.
3. 'Can the West be Converted?', Lesslie Newbiggin: *Mission and Units Digest*, March 1985, pp. 8, 9.
4. *The Power of the Powerless*, Jurgen Moltmann: SCM, p. 107.
5. *The Guardian*, 16th April 16th 1985.
6. 'For the Record', *Sojourners*, April 1985.

Chapter Three

The Church as a Sign of the Kingdom

The Church is a sign of the Kingdom, a sign that has often given confused and confusing signals. Among Western Christians, it is an open question as to what kind of kingdom is signalled by the Church. Among poor, disaffected and marginalised believers, the Church is seen as colluding with the powers that cause oppression and poverty. Many Christians, both rich and poor are asking the question: Is the Church a relevant and necessary sign of the Kingdom?

At the end of his ministry Jesus left women and men who had witnessed his life and miracles, and had heard in his teaching the intention to establish the Kingdom of God. From the trauma and dislocation that followed his execution, through the mystery of the resurrection experience and the letting go of the Ascension, these men and women became a distinctive community, whose declared allegiance was to Jesus as Lord and God. The Acts of the Apostles records the transformation of this group into a cohesive unit who spoke, without confusion, a message of repentance and commitment. This process of transformation, cohesion and courageous activity is recorded as the specific activity of the Spirit of God.

Following on the events of crucifixion and resurrection the 120 disciples kept a low profile. The reasons are not hard to find. The political atmosphere surrounding Jesus' death was electric. His execution was designed by the authorities to strike fear into the hearts of any would-be followers. Caiaphas, speaking for the religious lobby, saw Jesus' death as expedient and argued that 'one should die so that the whole nation should not perish' (John 5:50). Evidence of Roman brutality in quelling disorder was not hard to find, and government of this area of empire was frequently effected by force. For several weeks it looked as if the disciples would submit to the fear-inducement tactics of the authorities. Public witness to a discredited criminal was politically naive and personally suicidal. In human terms the Kingdom of God might have been ruled out by fear and the silencing of its witnesses. Had this been so, the message, life and death of Jesus would have been consigned to the dustbin of history as belonging to yet another failed revolutionary.

During the days in which the 120 were held hostage by fear to the governing authorities, the gathered community was becoming, unknown to itself, a sign, a Church. The Greek word for Church is 'ekklesia' which means 'gathered' or 'called out together'. They were to be a sign of the truth that, within historical circumstances apparently controlled by political and religious powers, God effects his purpose. Luke, the author of the Acts, records that all the believers 'were together in one place' (Acts 2:1). That *togetherness* was to be the first sign of the Church. It is reflected in a common lifestyle, shared possessions, worship and witness. The action of God in and through the events of Pentecost validates the principle declared by Jesus, 'I assign to you, as my father assigned to me, a kingdom' (Luke 22:37).

The pilgrims in Jerusalem during that Pentecost festival were profoundly affected by what they saw and heard. The disciples became the focus of world attention. Freed from fear, they courageously declared themselves to be *witnesses* of the resurrection of Jesus Christ. Publicly they revealed his life and work and spoke of him as 'a man attested to you by God with mighty works and wonders and signs which God did through him in your midst as you yourselves know'. His sentence and execution 'by the hands of lawless men' they spoke of fearlessly – hardly a wise move when referring to the Roman Governor and the military, not to mention the High Priest, Sanhedrin and Temple Guard! The spokesman, Peter, faced his hearers with the implications of the Jesus event and in particular the place of power and authority Jesus now carried 'at the right hand of God'. From this place he had poured out the Holy Spirit first on the disciples and then on all believers, so that his power and authority could influence all human experience.

The boldness and freedom with which Peter spoke were more indicative of a free-thinking democracy than a police state. His call to people 'to save themselves from this crooked generation' was both individual and corporate. All those listening would have been aware of the political pressure from the watching authorities. To respond to Peter's message was to choose an allegiance that would bring conflict and confrontation, whatever it offered of freedom and hope. The authorities initially acted cautiously with an occasional flogging and short term prison sentences (Acts 5:33–38). These were quickly followed by murder (Acts 7:58), plots to kill (Acts 9:29), persecution of minority groups (Acts 13:50), and assassination (Acts 12:2). This action reveals 'the Holy Spirit as a very political bird. The authoritative lines are crossed. Indeed, in Pentecost those lines are blown right off the spiritual map'.[1] In giving the Holy Spirit to believers, God's intention to establish his Kingdom is revealed in power. It will be a Kingdom that fulfils its promise 'to you and your children and all that are afar off, everyone whom the Lord our God calls to him' (Acts 2:39).

The communism of the Kingdom

The Church that had witnessed the Jesus event began to reveal the intention of God that it should be a sign of his Kingdom. Such a sign is born in political controversy and confrontation. Giving allegiance to the King and his Kingdom involves a

commitment to risk everything. The commitment to the
Kingdom is marked by repentance and baptism, the ensuing
risks are faced in fellowship rather than individualism.

The disciples' witness of the resurrection gave their message
integrity – because they had seen it they could talk about it.
Their lifestyle similarly had integrity, they were 'looked up to
by everyone' (Acts 2.47). The respect they had grew from the
quality and nature of their daily living which produced a rapid
growth within the embryonic Church. 'The Lord added day by
day to their number those who were being saved' (Acts 2.47).
The clear signals given by the believers enabled a positive
response from observers of these events.

The quality of life in the early Church was marked by what
Ernst Troeltsch[2] has called '*love communism*'. The holding of
all things in common; the selling of excess possessions; giving
to the needs of the poor; the vitality of their worship as well
as the sharing of meals and life together (Acts 2:42–47). The
early chapters of Acts are full of excitement and pace, reflecting
such idealism that some radical scholars doubt their authen-
ticity. Certainly Luke's language echoes the idealism of the
Greek philosophers. Martin Hengel[3] points out that the phrase
'they held all things in common' is reminiscent of the proverb
coined by Aristotle – 'The possession of friends is something
to be held in common'. It is important to know whether the
nature of the fellowship of the early Church was in some way
as recorded, with its attendant witness to Jesus, its political
status and the risks faced by its members, if it is to provide
clues on how the Church can be a sign of the Kingdom today.

Accounts of the early Church demonstrate the lasting effect
of Jesus' message. Jesus had spoken of the dangers of being
anxious, of 'unrighteous mammon', of possessions; he warned
against status and power among the citizens of the Kingdom.
He apparently had no place of his own, but shared the hospitality of others. (Though some have argued that he did have a
house in Capernaum, and to this were invited the outcasts and
the poor so often referred to in his parables.) He had told his

disciples that he would be returning soon. In the light of all of this the atheist philosopher Ernst Bloch[4] has argued that the love communism of the early Church was not just idealistic thinking by Luke, but a spiritual reality. Bloch believes that the love communism was both spontaneous and voluntary. 'It was not organised, nor was it subject to external compulsion. The decisive thing was "koinonia" not organisation. Secondly, Bloch contrasts the strictly organised and legalised sharing of goods evident in the rule of a contemporary Jewish monastic order, the Essene community. The idea was clearly that common possessions were meant to make "humiliating poverty" and "inordinate riches" impossible'.[5] The Essene example may well have been available to the Jerusalem community, but its emphasis on fellowship rather than law puts the Church on a different level altogether. Bloch's defence of the 'communism of love' concludes by referring to Jesus' teaching on possessions, money, status and his coming again. The early Church continued the carefree attitude of Jesus to the things of this world. Possessions have, throughout human experience, provided the source of human divisions. In the Kingdom they were no longer to be such an obstacle. 'No one said of his possessions that they belonged to him' simply became a further sign of the Kingdom.

It is said that the 'love communism' of the early Christian community was only practised in Jerusalem until the time of the famine of the AD 40's, when the whole experiment was given up. This does not appear to be so. Paul and Barnabas frequently raised money for the Church in Jerusalem.

Jerusalem was not alone in its practice of love communism as Barnabas reveals. He is a significant figure in our understanding of the practice of sharing. Barnabas was a Levite and a Cypriot. Along with other landowners he had sold his land for the well being of all. Hengel[6] tells us that Barnabas was known by the Church at Antioch by whom the tradition of love communism was preserved, indicating that it was practised widely in the early Church. 'The Church (at Antioch) proudly pointed to him as an authority who had himself had a part in the "love communism" of the early Church. This note (Acts 4:36) is presumably one of the references to Luke's Antiochene source.'[7]

The Jerusalem community was not without its tensions as it lived its common life of sharing, worship and the breaking of bread. Mealtimes brought a mixed bunch to the table, a place where boundaries of culture, class, sex and race were frequently crossed. Prostitutes, Samaritans, the poor and the outcasts of society ate with Jesus. It is not surprising then that in such a mixed community the first hassles appear over food distribution. The Greek members complained that their widows were being discriminated against by the Hebrew members in the daily share out (Acts 6:1ff). Disputes had to be quickly settled by the apostles. Unity around the table was integral to Eastern family life anyway, but was fundamental to the shared life of the community in the eyes of onlookers. Paul had to give his attention to a similar situation in Corinth some time later (1 Corinthians 11:17–33).

The quality of public living of the ecclesia inspired thousands of people to take steps to enter the Kingdom of God. The birth of the Church as a sign of the Kingdom crossed all cultural, racial, sexual and class frontiers. It laid itself open to confrontation with the surrounding political, social, religious and economic powers. By the power of the Spirit the Church proclaimed the kingship of Christ; it called for a turning away from the values and attitudes of the age, and for repentance from the people who manipulated those attitudes and values. The quality of its 'koinonia' gave it an integrity that was above reproach. Both leadership and membership accepted the disciplines of love. Its life was a reflection of Pentecost, the festival of the first fruits of the harvest. By the fruit it bore in its life, the early Church was giving unmistakable signs of the Kingdom.

This Church was a community and was seen as a community. It was truly communitarian. It was a Church that understood its message and read the signs of the times, and as such was prophetic. It was a Church that freed people to enjoy the forgiveness and the power of God, opening them up to love that transformed all aspects of life and relationships. It was a liberated and liberating community. Its life was lived in the urgency of its founder who in his first sermon said 'Repent, for the Kingdom of heaven is at hand' (Matthew 4:17).

Such insight into the lifestyle and environment of the early Christian community should leave modern Christians asking in what ways, and to what extent should the early Church be regarded as a pattern for the Church today?

An American Indian speaking to a conference of clergy, lay workers and theologians in New York several years ago said, 'Regardless of what the New Testament says most Christians are materialists with no experience of the Spirit, and mostly Christians are individualists with no real commitment to community. Let's pretend that you all were Christians. You would not accumulate, you would actually love one another, you would share everything that you had with one another and with the poor, and you would treat each other as if you were family.' He concluded his remarks with a question: 'What is it that keeps you from doing that?' An observer at the conference remarked that no one had a good answer to that question.

Such a challenge is pertinent to the Church in the West. Individualism, and affluence, with an over-dependence on materialism, make it a prime target for such criticism. The Church among the poor has a greater commitment to community and to the sharing of life and possessions. The fellowship of the poor regards each as belonging to one family. For the Church to be a sign of the Kingdom must it be committed to the poor, to community and to shared life?

Among the Church of the poor a theology and spirituality of liberation is developing. It is biblically rooted, and therefore demands careful attention. One of its basic tenets is that in order for the Church to be a sign of the Kingdom it has to be committed to the poor. Gustavo Gutierrez says that 'the teaching of Jesus is framed in a context that moves from "poor to the poor" '. He shows how in Matthew's gospel, the opening chapters deal with the birth and the preparation of Jesus for his mission, while the last three chapters deal with his death as a result of that mission, and the resurrection. 'The twenty-one chapters in between these two sections give us the preaching of Jesus. They begin with the blessing of the poor (Matthew 5): they end with the assertion that we meet Christ himself when we go out to the poor with concrete acts – feeding the hungry, clothing the naked, sheltering the homeless and visiting the imprisoned (Matthew 25). The poor and the Kingdom are linked realities. It is in their relationship that the Father's gratuitous love is revealed'.[8]

The King and His Kingdom

'In and as Jesus the Kingdom came,' writes David Jenkins. 'He is the man whose obedience was the Kingdom, for God was in Christ reconciling the world to himself, declaring the power of the Kingdom, making plain the presence of the Kingdom and totally underwriting the promise of the Kingdom.'[9] It follows that disciples of Jesus must be loyal to the practice of Jesus. The Kingdom is a gift of grace but as such it makes demands. Matthew frequently makes the point that the Kingdom is the judge of the community of disciples, the Church. 'You will know them by their fruits' (Matthew 7:20). And, as Gutierrez emphasises, 'these fruits are technically described in the Bible as "works of mercy", or "good works". They are concrete acts on behalf of the poor: e.g. offering food and drink. The characteristic thing about Matthew's Gospel which gives definitive force to this criterion, is the assertion that in these works on behalf of the poor we encounter Christ. That ultimately is what grace is.'[10]

The Kingdom of God judges the Church, and the world judges the Church, and if the gifts of the Kingdom are not visible in fruit borne then its witness is invalidated (1 Corinthians 13:1–3). The world judges the Kingdom by what it sees in the Church. The world judges the God of the Kingdom by what it sees of its citizens. The way the Church understands God has a direct bearing on how it reflects the Kingdom.

Biblically there has always been a tension between God as 'wholly other' and 'God with us'. The Jews as a nation were frequently under threat of conquest, dispersion and annihilation. God had to be seen as acting within history as liberator from slavery, conqueror in battle, bringer of good harvests. Such signs vindicated their faith in a God who could not be seen, alongside the evident symbols of the localised gods of neighbouring tribes and conquerors. To a people whose perception of life and death was limited God had to be a God of the here and now. Towards the end of the Old Testament experience two strands of thinking about God began to develop: the perception of God as one who suffers with and for his people; and the idea of hope in some final vindication beyond the experience of the here and now. A strong mystical, 'personal' element of faith developed during the exilic years and after, leading to the excesses of Pharisaism during the time of Jesus.

The heart of Christian proclamation is 'God is King'. The God who is King is the God and Father of our Lord Jesus Christ. He is a King who associates with his subjects, and who, in Jesus, reveals his compassion and love. The Kingdom that he rules is both present and future. It is a Kingdom that is worldwide, but whose actual limits are those of the cosmos. It is a Kingdom that operates within human history, in the past and the present, and which will ultimately make sense of both past and present. In the history of the Jews, God's covenant people, he reveals himself as a God of justice and life (Isaiah 30:18, Psalm 37:28, Deuteronomy 10:18).

The Hebrew name for this God, 'Go'el', means the one who defends the poor and oppressed. When we make him less than he declares himself to be we reduce him to the god of our own perceptions and make him an idol. Western Christianity with its over-emphasis on individualism and its absorption with materialism has been in danger of separating God from his Kingdom and its demands and thereby falling into idolatry.

There is truth in the thinking that says the way we understand God is a reflection of the way we understand ourselves. The Victorian understanding of the father in the family was as a remote, austere and at times brutal figure. The imagery of God which this produced is still left in much of our sub-conscious. Father was to be feared, God is to be feared. Put in another way, our classical perception of God is of an all-powerful, all-knowing Being. Beside such a God, human beings are limited both by life-span and knowledge. God is hard to identify with, because he is so great.

If we get stuck with the idea that God is omniscient and omnipotent, then it follows that he is only to be experienced in mystery, as wholly other. All relationships with him will then be interpreted from the place of inadequacy and sinfulness, not from the glory of a created being. When God is separated from the history and experience of his people he remains forever 'out there', or 'in my heart' locked away from any objective reality. Jesus' life, death and resurrection then remain as experiences that once happened, rather than events that continue within the history of humankind.

The liberator of the Kingdom

Among the poor God is understood as One who liberates, not only from personal sin, but from institutionalised sin expressed in poverty, oppression, brutality and marginalisation. He is known as a God who suffers hardships with all who are oppressed. Believers join together in solidarity to bear whatever may be done to them. 'Living out . . . faith amid those struggles enables . . . a different perspective'. Phrases such as 'God the liberator', 'God the life', or 'the black God' are born out of suffering and hope. 'These are deeply lived experiences which are celebrated with paschal joy. They pass through death to affirm life.'[11] Death and resurrection are not seen simply as historical events, or as salvation history, but common experiences of all God's people at all times and in all circumstances.

It is something of this perspective that the Church needs to grasp in the West if it is to become a relevant sign of the Kingdom. To do this its leaders and people have to be convinced that in Western society, poverty, discrimination and oppression not only exist but are actually, or tacitly, approved by governments. Many in British society experience threats to and violations of their civil liberties and human rights. This is particularly so among the unemployed, blacks, Asians and prisoners. Much of the social unrest in Northern Ireland, and in the flashpoints of Brixton, London; Toxteth, Liverpool; Mosside, Manchester; and Handsworth, Birmingham have been fuelled by the failure of successive governments to deal with the underlying causes so often manifested in unemployment, bad housing, poor schooling and developing racial ghettos.

Methods of repression, rather than re-evaluation of policies have been used to keep people subject to the law of the land without due regard for basic moral and human rights. Economically there is a polarisation between the 'haves' and 'have-nots' in Britain while in international affairs, rich nations take steps to protect their own interests while exploiting and placing at risk whole sections not only of their own population but of the world at large.

To face such reality in the Western Church means to face up to the need for solidarity with the poor and marginalised. Solidarity, many now see as a word which expresses the Hebrew idea of collectivity.[12] Solidarity is about belonging, and in that belonging believing that what happens to one or some, affects all. As Paul puts it, 'If one member suffers, all suffer together; if one member is honoured all rejoice together' (1 Corinthians 12:26). Moltmann strongly respects this concept as a socialist word and perception, but he asks, 'Is solidarity, the word and the concept another expression for the Christian way of life too, and for the motives behind Christian action?'[13]

Jim Wallis, peace activist, Church renewal leader, and convenor of Sojourners community in Washington believes that solidarity is the key to Christian influence and action. He gives to solidarity a more familiar biblical word which he feels needs rehabilitating, the word 'Koinonia' or fellowship. He simply states 'the call to love one another and to offer our lives for the sake of the world. The creation of living, breathing, loving communities of faith at the local Church level is the foundation for all our answers'.[14] It sounds simple to the point of being naive but it was, as we have seen, the way of life that marked out the influence of the early Church upon the society in which it was set. There will of course be cultural, historical and sociological differences to contend with but the foundational principle of 'koinonia' remains.

As Westerners with our emphasis upon the individual in achievement, moral behaviour, choice, religious faith and so on, the concept of solidarity, collective identity and responsibility remains outside most of our experience. Yet with independence and individualism go the two major features of isolation and loneliness evident in Western Church and society.

Working towards any sense of interdependence or solidarity means facing implications of the Lordship of Christ. Many individuals struggle gamely with the Lordship of Christ in their daily living, and most fail to experience it. Most Christian experience in reality, if not in theory, is about going it alone. After conversion most people are left to make sense of 'God, the Universe and everything else', on their own. We have a 'scalp-taking' view of conversion. Once 'saved', conversion is complete. An ongoing spiritual life of prayer, meditation on the scriptures and worship, is divorced from attitudes to work, questions of political allegiance, the use of our leisure and the development of our relationships.

Jim Wallis is helpful here. He sees conversion as 'the translation of persons from one world to another. It is inviting them into an environment where it becomes possible to live a

Christian life'. He is not arguing escapism from the world, but he looks to community for strength to encounter it.

'We have to create a base that is internally strong enough to enable us to survive as Christians and to empower us to be actively engaged in the world. The community becomes the place where the healing of our own lives becomes the foundation for the healing of the nations. The making of community is finally the only thing strong enough to resist the system and to provide an adequate spiritual foundation for better and more human ways to live.'[15]

The creation of community and the emergence of solidarity are at the heart of the struggle for the Church to become a sign of the Kingdom. We need some models, and these we must now look at, both in the UK, in the basic communities of Central and Southern America and elsewhere.

Notes

1. Bill Kellerman: *Sojourners*, 1985.
2. *Property and riches in the early Church*, Martin Hengel: SCM, p. 31.
3. *Ibid.*, p. 31.
4. *Ibid.*, p. 32.
5. *Ibid.*, p. 33.
6. *Ibid.*, p. 33.
7. *Ibid.*, p. 33.
8. 'Challenge of Basic Christian Communities', Gustavo Gutierrez: *The Poor and Christian Communities*, p. 121.
9. 'Kingdom and Agenda', David Jenkins: *Mission and Unity* Digest Issue 28, July 1985.
10. Gutierrez, *op cit.*, p. 121.
11. Gutierrez, *op cit.*, p. 123.
12. The theme of solidarity is developed in Albert Nolan's *Jesus Before Christianity:* Darton Longman and Todd.
13. *Power of the Powerless*, Jurgen Moltmann: SCM, p. 107.
14. Jim Wallis: *Sojourners*, January 1980.
15. Jim Wallis: *Sojourners*, January 1980.

Chapter Four

A Church Running Against the Tide?

Jean Vanier, founder leader of L'Arche, a community working with mentally handicapped people, has described a Christian community as 'one that will always be running against the tide of society, with its individualistic values of wealth and comfort and resulting rejection of the people who get in the way of these. A Christian community constantly calls its members to share, welcome, become poorer and go beyond their resources to a truer love.'[1] For many Christian people such a description is an ideal, something we believe in as dogma but which we feel to be unobtainable. Yet 'koinonia' is revealed in the New Testament as the distinctive sign of the Church in its witness to the Kingdom. It is a unique blend of compassion, solidarity, obedience and servanthood. The Church's task is to make its life visibly distinctive by its sharing, its welcome of others, its poverty and self-sacrifice. When it lives like this, it becomes discomforting and disconcerting; it produces strong reactions which polarise in commitment or persecution.

The distinctive element of the early Christian community was its quality of life. How Christians behaved towards each other was very important. 'There must be no competition among you, no conceit; but everybody is to be self-effacing. Always consider the other person to be better than yourself, so that nobody thinks of his own interests first but everybody thinks of other people's interests instead' (Philippians 2:3–4 JB).

This lifestyle grew out of intimacy and integrity and was one in which no one regarded things as their own. It saw the greater good of the community as being above personal achievement. This quality of life grew from a common experience of suffering, isolation and loneliness experienced by its members. The Jewish faith was hostile to the early Christian and the prevailing Roman government ruthlessly crushed any signs of dissent.

Confusion and allegiance

In the West there is a confusion of allegiance among Christians. Society is often described as 'Christian'. The idea that we live in a 'Christian country' has been allowed to prevail. In the UK the existence of the Established Church has contributed to this misconception. Christian values and precepts may be called into play at moments of national moral indignation, but the pervasive philosophy of the West is a self-interested humanism. Such a philosophy has prevailed in the Church, mirroring as it does the society in which it is set.

Lesslie Newbiggin has described British Christianity as in 'an advanced state of syncretism'. The reason is that 'the Church has lived so long as a permitted and even privileged minority, accepting relegation to the private sphere in a culture whose public life is controlled by a totally different vision of reality, that it has almost lost the power to address a radical challenge to that vision and therefore to modern Western civilisation as a whole'.[2]

The greater part of our life is spent finding security and safety. Where our security is, there our loyalty will tend to be also. Jesus recognised the need for security, and saw how it called forth loyalties which put membership of the Kingdom of God at risk. He states, 'Do not lay up for yourselves treasures on earth . . . but lay up for yourselves treasures in heaven . . .

For where your treasure is, there will your heart be also'
(Matthew 6:19–22). Treasure and loyalties are synonymous.

People give their allegiance to the places and people with
whom their security is most assured. Employers call for
considerable commitment from employees, particularly those
in the higher echelons of management, or of government, with
the promise of reward and security. But it is not only managers
and government officials or even retainers of long established
companies who are bound up in giving loyalty to the place of
security. Newbiggin puts his finger on the 'nation state' as the
'entity to which ultimate loyalty is due . . . in the twentieth
century we have become accustomed to the fact that – in the
name of the nation – Catholics will fight Catholics, Protestants
will fight Protestants, and Marxists will fight Marxists. The
charge of blasphemy, if it is ever made, is treated as a quaint
anachronism; but the charge of treason, of placing another
loyalty above that of the nation state is treated as an unforgivable crime. The nation state has taken the place of God . . .
National governments are widely assumed to be responsible for
and capable of providing those things which former generations
thought only God could provide – freedom from fear, hunger,
diseases and want – in a word: happiness.'[3]

Rediscovering allegiance to God

To rediscover allegiance to God and to find him as the place
of security and the source of true happiness is the task for all
who claim citizenship of the Kingdom of God. The conflict and
anguish involved in such a transference of allegiance, loyalty
and security is integral to the whole Bible story. Abraham is
revealed as a man of faith because of his willingness to leave
the security of Ur, its culture, wealth and status, for the
insecurity of a nomadic existence in a hostile land – his only
security the promise of God to be with him and to make of
him a great nation.

Transferring loyalty and risking security for an unknown and untested environment on the basis of a promise is costly, if not foolhardy. Yet that is what allegiance to the Kingdom of God demands. God does not want us to take these risks in isolation. He has provided us with an environment of security and safety, although there is precious little evidence of its existence within our Churches. Christian fellowship is seen by many as a place of refuge, of safety from the world, even a place for one's own healing and of learning and growing in the faith. While all that is so, the Church is rarely seen as a place of economic support and an environment in which people are deprogrammed from the loyalties that keep them from being citizens of the Kingdom. The depth of our encounters with God and one another in the Church should fit us to bring about the healing of the world. The Kingdom of God is not an escape route from the world, but a community from which ambassadors are sent with the task of announcing and making reconciliation possible (2 Corinthians 5:11–21).

Conversion should be a process by which people move from one environment into another. Those who were first converted through the preaching of the apostles began a new life together in the community. It was this togetherness that marked them out (Acts 2:42–47), and enabled them to bear the sufferings which were to come upon them as a community. It was this same togetherness that enabled them to confront an oppressive and hostile world.

The world in which we live is no less hostile and oppressive. Although many of us in the West do not experience its oppressive nature our brothers and sisters in Christ in South Africa, Ethiopia and under communist and fascist regimes do. Our homes are filled daily with the litany of human suffering and pain. Our reactions to the news are complex. Sometimes we feel helpless, more often we feel angry and frightened. As individuals there is little that we can do but gape on in horror or turn away. Occasionally our response will be generous as some Bob Geldof inspires us to an event like the 'Live Aid

Concert' and we give because at last there is something we can do.

Jesus was moved with compassion for the hungry (Matthew 14:4) and asks us to follow his example. He spoke of his 'yoke being easy and his burden light' (Matthew 11:30), but for many Christians his demands seem heavy, overbearing and impossible. Jesus promised that his followers would do greater miracles than he had done (John 14:2) but evidence of them is hard to find. His followers are to be people of humility and gentleness of heart (Matthew 11:29), people marked out by the quality of their life: distinct and sure, free from anxiety, available for others. To be like this is not something within the grasp of most individuals. It is something that has to be learned, through our experience with others. Christian people will not, in isolation, make effective lovers of the world God loved so much. The love God asks of us is a love in solidarity and struggle with others. To experience it demands a revolution in our thinking about koinonia – fellowship.

Community . . . root of compassion

Henri Nouwen in his many studies of Christian witness and relationships is convinced that 'wherever true Christian community is formed, compassion happens in the world . . . Since it is in community that God's compassion reveals itself, solidarity, servanthood and obedience, are also the main characteristics of our life together. Solidarity can hardly be an individual accomplishment. It is difficult for us as individuals to enter into the pains and sufferings of our fellow human beings. But in the community gathered in Christ's name there is an unlimited space into which strangers from different places with very different stories can enter and experience God's compassionate presence.'[4]

By and large our Churches are not places where strangers are welcome. Neither are they places where we enter into the pains of our fellow human beings. We are not very good at entering into suffering by proxy. Does this mean that the Western Church has to wait for some holocaust or catastrophe in order to become a place of solidarity, a community of people who are prepared to confront, with the reconciling gospel of Christ, the powers that threaten to obliviate compassion and love in our world? Certainly the communities of faith that seem to be bearing most effective witness to the power of Christ and his reconciling love are those that have endured suffering and oppression. Other groups, like Sojourners in Washington DC, and L'Arche with its work among the mentally handicapped, have read the signs of the times and have sought to live out their lives in a defiant 'yes' to the gospel. In the face of nuclear annihilation, oppressive regimes and the breakdown of society such groups proclaim the coming Kingdom of God. Almost without exception communities that run against the tide of society and reveal compassion in the world, are formed in the midst of conflict. In the UK little groups of people in Northern Ireland are working for reconciliation and hope in a society torn apart by civil war.

Ulster – Community disintegrating

Ulster has been a place of conflict brought all too frequently to our attention over the past sixteen years. The roots of the conflict are deep and intertwined. On the one hand they are racial in origin: conquest and subjugation of the native Irish by the English; the settling of the North by emigrating Scots and the subsequent uprisings which culminated in the founding of Eire and the division into North and South in 1922. On the other hand the problem is religious; a problem highlighted in the North by the immigrants from Scotland who tended to be Covenanters or Presbyterians, while the indigenous population was Catholic. The problem is also one of ideology; the socialist aspirations of traditional Irish nationalism mingle uncomfortably with the Marxist intentions of Provisional Sinn Fein, and clash violently with the conservatism of Unionists and the fascist tendencies of more extreme loyalists. While class is not obviously the most Irish of divisions, affluence and poverty are, and this too contributes to the confusion of the situation.

To look at Northern Ireland is to see a microcosm of the way in which loyalty to the nation state has taken the place of God. The nation state for the loyalist is a self-governing Protestant province within the United Kingdom. Such a hope springs from statements like that of Clifford Smyth, a member of the Democratic Unionist Party: 'The story of the plantation of Ulster is underwritten by the Almighty hand of God.' Or less prosaically lived out in the spirit of Billy Mitchell of the Ulster Volunteer Force: 'I may be a bad Christian but I am a good Protestant.'

Republicans idealise a united Ireland and allegiance to the struggle to free Ireland from foreign domination, namely British. As Eamonn McCann from Derry's Bogside put it, 'We came very early to our politics. One learned literally from one's mother's knee that Christ died for the human race and Padraig Pearse for the Irish section of it.'

Both communities carry out their cause to a greater or lesser extent in the name of God, but fail to recognise the intrinsic blasphemy of that claim. The aggressive fundamentalism of Ian Paisley with its roots in personal salvation and private faith has been elevated to a crusade for a 'Moral Majority' style government in Northern Ireland. With the relocation of many people from inner city to suburbs, the heartland of Paisley's support, once almost exclusively the poor and working class, has shifted to the glens of Antrim and the affluent and influential farming communities. Catholic priests working on the largely modern housing estates of Northern Irish cities have seen the troubles as a fight against oppression and a struggle for liberation. Frequently that cause has become bound up with the intentions, if not the practices, of the IRA.

The British Government, in its concern with the political reality of Northern Ireland, takes little account of the Christianity of either side. The economic and political strain of

Northern Ireland upon successive governments makes it a problem to be resolved in the most expedient way. If God can be used to resolve the situation, he will be, but if not he will be dispensed with. God, in the last resort, has become an expendable or exploitable commodity.

In 1969 Connor Cruse O'Brien commented, 'Just as in the Republic the aspiration to acquire Northern Ireland is a low intensity aspiration, so in Great Britain the aspiration to get rid of Northern Ireland is a low priority aspiration. Both have therefore low priorities in terms of practical politics.'

Since the troubles began in 1968 the Christian Church in Ireland has been in turmoil. From the rioting and burning of Belfast, Derry and Armagh came the polarisation of the communities. There was a mass migration across the cities to the traditional ghettos under the Union Jack or the Tricolour. This polarisation and fragmentation remains as a legacy of the holocaust of the 'sixties and 'seventies. Within the ghettos in which many sought refuge, the tyranny of the paramilitaries and the processes of fear and intimidation made safety a relative virtue.

Family life has been placed under enormous strain. That strain continues and is expressed most painfully in mixed Catholic and Protestant marriages, where people are frequently unwelcome in either community. Enforced movements meant the loss of jobs, and fear of assassination or attack led many into permanent unemployment because of the danger of crossing sectarian boundaries. The Troubles themselves increased unemployment in what was already an economically fragile community. Children suffered in their schooling, and many showed signs of psychological and psychosomatic disorders. In the Church, as in politics, the centre was decimated. In the early days concerned Church people dashed around like firemen trying to quench flames, and dampen smouldering violence. Much quiet and unrecognised work was done during that period, without which the situation would undoubtedly have been worse. Even so, the fruits of mistrust, prejudice and suspicion grew so fast into polarisation that any values of kindness and goodness were bound to be shortlived. The Church of Ireland, Baptists, Methodists and others have substantially kept out of the political arena, confining themselves to ritualistic denunciations of terrorist violence. In recent years a more radical Catholic voice has been raised, epitomised in Bishop Cahill Dealy of Belfast who has condemned IRA violence unequivocally.

The situation is one of great complexity and confusion. The two religious groupings have other significant differences, and in these lie the roots of their conflict. Protestantism is the religion of respectability and righteousness. It is the religion of the conqueror. Catholicism is essentially primitive in Ireland, it is tied to the land and the struggle for survival. Both groups, because of their history, are grounded in fear and hatred. In Ulster Christ's body is dismembered before our very eyes centuries after his physical mutilation and death. This division spills over into violence and God in his humanity is once again murdered by humanity. It is shockingly true that hatred rather than love is the dominant expression of Christian people in defence of their traditions.

The hunger strikes of the late 1970s and early 1980s reveal that mutilation and starvation are not just modes of martyrdom, but also deep expressions of felt unworthiness. Irish Catholicism with its emphasis on sin, penance, purgatory and punishment before glory, produces a self-hatred. Punishment, self-inflicted or imposed does not cure it, but instinctively it is felt that it may help to purge the soul. Roman Catholics in Ulster have felt isolated, powerless, downtrodden and helpless. Such helplessness has intensified their hatred of the self and subsequently of the oppressor.

Protestantism in Ulster is founded on the idea of a justifying God. To many he is one who justifies the good while hating and destroying the bad. The bad are all those who cannot see God or good in the way 'we can'. From such a view springs another kind of hatred which is described by Thomas Merton as hatred that 'enjoys the pleasure of hating for it is directed towards the unworthiness of the other . . . it is a hate that is strong because it does not believe itself to be unworthy and alone'.[5] Such hatred expresses itself in people in one of two ways: either by being blind to one's own faults and seeing the fault only in others; or, by being 'aware of his own unworthiness and the unworthiness of his brother he is tempted with a subtler and more tormenting kind of hate; the general, searing, nauseating hatred of everything and everyone because everything is tainted with unworthiness, everything is unclean and foul with sin'.[6] So, the Protestant preacher denounces Catholicism and his own congregation in one and the same sermon. Ulster Protestantism is schizophrenic because it manages to exercise both aspects of its hatred in quite separate boxes.

Intentional Community – signs of hope

To the casual observer signs of hope are few and there is an enormous resignation to the continuation of violence and division. There are however some exceptions, real signs of hope, community and compassion. There is a growing movement for peace and reconciliation. Much of the work has been spearheaded by movements such as Corrymeela, a community of Catholics and Protestants founded in the mid-sixties and 'dedicated to the fostering of better understanding of men and women not only in Ireland but far beyond'.[7] Although conceived before the events of 1968, 'Corrymeela was overtaken by events but never overwhelmed by them. For fifteen years Corrymeela has opened its doors to all comers – to the tired, the maimed, the bewildered and the embittered; to the Christian, to the Agnostic, to the Atheist. It has tried to comfort the afflicted and challenge the comfortable.'[8]

Corrymeela community works in its centre at Ballycastle as well as in towns and cities across the province. Its lifestyle is not deliberately simple, but it is based around a simple covenant and commitment to work together for reconciliation. Its work and influence is much greater than the sum total of its members and associates. Much of its work involves facilitating groups, enabling people who want and need to meet each other to do so. Visiting Belfast in 1985 I came across such a group of ordinary Catholics and Protestants who had decided to work together for peace and their children. Their meetings were held at great personal risk, and Corrymeela along with Cornerstone, one of an increasing number of low profile communities, was facilitating their meetings.

Such communities and reconciliation groups have come from a place of brokenness. They look to a hope not for themselves but for their children and grandchildren. All have experienced the devastation and isolation which the years of the Troubles have brought to Ulster. The opening words of one community covenant acknowledge this: 'Today we are broken, we are needing, we do not feel one people.'[9]

During the early seventies people from both sides of the divide sought to understand their situation in terms that were reminiscent of the Exodus: 'I have heard the cry of my people . . . I will deliver them from the hands of oppression'. This phrase, often quoted by Mary Grant of Cornerstone Community, reflected the pain people faced within themselves, their community and in their society. She said, 'The situation frequently left us with the question, "Is there anything there?" ' Understanding the cry of the people meant facing into disillusionment, failure and doubt in an honest way. It meant placing those experiences alongside the occasions when some hope for renewal was also expressed in the experience of an overwhelming sense of God's love.

This process of renewal reflects a refusal to be 'conformed to this world' and a willingness to be 'transformed by the renewal of the mind' (Romans 12:2 adapted). Such a renewal of mind is paramount and John Morrow of Corrymeela sees it as the priority work of reconciliation. Many, he believes, have 'emigrated with their minds' – all those who will not or cannot apply their minds to countering propaganda and prejudice spewing out of extremists from all sides.

Cells of reconciliation

Small cells of people, frequently emanating from main stream Churches but deliberately ecumenical, have formed into small communities committed to sharing resources at various different levels. They face the implications of the question 'Who in this situation, is God for us?' Many have taken courageous steps in rejecting the traditional gods of Nationalism or Loyalism, the nation state in its various forms. They have recognised the limitations of security in physical and material terms, and have dared to offer love to the places of hatred and fear which they have discovered both within themselves, and on their own and the other side of the divide.

With the passage of time the question has become 'How much does God mean to us in the place where we are?' For every step of growing together, every act of reconciliation and peacemaking, is marked by a re-evaluation of who and what people are to each other. Within the communities a state of thinking has grown up which Mary Grant has described as 'being held somewhere between Good Friday and Easter Day in our lives. It is one event yet we live in the interminable time in between'.

Practically, this has meant a simple sharing of experience of life. Testimony to faith in Jesus Christ and insights into scripture are all honestly, unjudgingly and unhurriedly listened to and shared. It has meant the development of liturgy and prayer; the sharing of goods, resources and talents. It has meant creating an environment where it is safe to be Christian without first of all deciding what kind. The cells and communities have become places of hope for the wider neighbourhood, as they seek to tackle places of stress – unemployment, family crises, intimidation, membership of the paramilitaries and so on. These small communities are submitting to a continual process of conversion and a form of repentance that is an opening up of the self to the healing love of God.

None of this has been won cheaply. Reconciliation is not simple or easy, it is not about papering over cracks and ignoring reality. It begins at the place of mutual brokenness, of devastation. The New Testament reveals the basic action of God in Christ as that of reconciliation. He 'reconciles all things to himself whether on earth or in heaven, making peace by the blood of the cross' (Colossians 1:20). The cross reveals supremely the God of love; a God not of vengeance but of pity. A God who suffers the cruelty of his own creation with a quality of love that conquers hatred and death. A love that loves worthy and unworthy alike. The common experience of those involved in reconciliation in Northern Ireland is the decision to believe that reconciliation lies at the heart of the God and Father of our Lord Jesus Christ and they will not be put off by imitations. This decision has produced a conscious acknowledgement that Jesus Christ is the Lord of all life, not just the personal aspects.

Reconciliation – new structures, new people

Two pictures of reconciliation emerge in the New Testament. One is the image of a building that has been destroyed to its very foundations, with a new building constructed stone by stone on the site of the old. In the wasteland of much that is Northern Ireland such an image is powerful and accurate. The need for prejudice, fear, hatred, anger, bitterness, violence, lust, greed and war to be annihilated is clear. To hope and work for a new structure built on love, peace, patience, gentleness, kindness, self-control is evident.

The second picture is that of an exchange; the exchanging of 'many selves' for 'one self'. Reconciliation literally means to become one self. Such an exchange is a struggle. It is a struggle within the individual, but it is equally a struggle within the community. It is a struggle that touches public, religious, political and personal life. It is a struggle that brings about the reconciliation of all things in Jesus Christ.

From this struggle has come a hope and a challenge. The hope is that the Church can be a really effective instrument, the kind which Paul envisages in his letter to the Ephesians, a Church that bears witness to the wisdom and purpose of God. 'So that the Sovereignties and Powers should learn, only now, through the Church how comprehensive God's wisdom really is exactly according to the plan which he had from all eternity in Christ Jesus our Lord' (Ephesians 3:10, 11 JB).

The experience of Christian communities in Ulster challenges all established Churches. They have discovered God acting in their own story and history. As the events of Ulster have broken and renewed people so the historical events of the life, death and resurrection of Jesus Christ have become contemporary in their own experience. Within that same experience has grown a resistance to all the things that contradict the claims of Jesus. It is a resistance that faces the possibility of counter-resistance, and even persecution. Such a possibility was illustrated all too clearly when several years ago Mother Theresa visited Belfast. Seeking to begin some work of reconciliation at the heart of the divide, she was, after a few days, approached by a representative of the Security Forces who asked her to leave. 'Mother,' he said, 'we cannot take your kind of loving here.' From that apparently abortive visit much of what happens now was inspired, but the story serves to remind of the risk and the cost.

The experience of communities in Northern Ireland reveal a Church set free to be a liberating and healing body. A place where people not only hear the gospel but experience it. A place where those who suffer because of the divisions of society are being healed. A place where those who have had no dignity and have known the crushing weight of oppression, are recognised and given dignity and rights. It is a Church that frees people to be at home within it, and a Church that has found its place among the poor. As in all struggles, so in the Irish struggle, it is the poor who have suffered. The people who are being freed to be at home in the intentional Christian communities are those at the bottom of things. Such a movement challenges the Church to rediscover its roots among those who are most deprived and marginalised.

This movement carries with it the responsibility of being prophetic. It calls for conversion which is both personal and public. It challenges the Church, society and governments with the need to change. It recognises people's need for a common life in which their humanity can be shared in worshipping God together.

It calls away from individualism and lack of commitment, to a fresh vision of Jesus as Lord, having 'disarmed the principalities and powers and made a public example of them, triumphing over them' (Colossians 3:15).

Risking being vulnerable

To accept such a challenge means becoming vulnerable. It involves the Church recognising in groups, congregations and synods that because of our privileged minority position we have not run against the tide of society. It means repenting of a preference for the individualistic values of wealth and comfort, and a rejection of the movement to upward social mobility. It means Church members making conscious choices to share themselves, their resources, salaries and employment opportunities. Above all it means discovering new ways of sharing our worship, our prayer and our study of God's word. Such a vulnerability calls us to welcome the stranger, the poor and the needy.

To risk opening ourselves to others, sharing our weaknesses pain and failure as well as our hopes and aspirations, is hard. Yet it is essential for the kind of fellowship that goes beyond the polite, careful, guarded relationships that so often pass for love within our Churches. We fear vulnerability because we would risk others taking advantage of us and we rightly do not want to be taken advantage of. The experience of communities in Ulster, however, is that external events viciously exposed the weaknesses and nakedness of all. Both individuals and whole sections of the population felt themselves deeply shamed by the events that overtook the province. The poverty of love and the failure to live the gospel was revealed to everyone. A few people began to see that suffering was the common experience of all and that individuals were helpless to resist the forces of darkness. It was in joining with others and sharing common wounds and pain that true compassion emerged. Vulnerability was expressed in compassion.

The cross of Jesus reveals the nakedness of God. He is totally vulnerable. His compassion and his identity are with human beings in their suffering and pain. By his death on the cross Jesus opened 'an unlimited space' (the Old Testament understanding of salvation) for strangers from different places with different stories to enter his presence. Such vulnerability is necessary among God's people if they are to be a sign of hope for others. We need to create 'an unlimited space' within the life of our Churches.

If the Church is to effectively 'run against the tide of society', we need to face the reality of the allegiances we hold over and above our allegiance to God – loyalty to the nation state and our dependence upon self-interested humanistic governments being two primary areas. We need to recognise the idols we have worshipped in allowing, as we do, the state to play the role of God; offering us at a price, freedom from fear, hunger, disease, war and want. We need to recognise institutional wickedness as well as personal sin. The causes as well as the prevention of public disorder and unrest should be the concern of the Church. We need to recognise the extent to which we have been 'conformed to this world', and accept that part of the process of repentance is the opening of ourselves to the 'renewal of our minds' in our attitudes and allegiance.

The experience of Ulster reveals in microcosm the dangers that lie below the surface of life in the United Kingdom and in the West as a whole. We cannot assume that we shall continue in a society of relative security and affluence, for the prejudices which have surfaced and found expression in the anger and violence of Ulster, and on the streets of Handsworth and Brixton, are prevalent both in Church and the rest of society. Such prejudice is born out of fear. Fear is the root of anger, and anger the propellant of violence. A thin veil of respectability masks our fears within Church and society. What passes for peace is in reality little more than armed neutrality.

The model of hope Jean Vanier challenges us with is one that calls for a people willing to take risks in working against the tide of society, developing ways of sharing, welcoming, becoming poorer as well as going beyond our normal human resources in order to reveal 'a truer love'. Small groups in Northern Ireland are discovering that model and becoming a sign of a way of living that is communitarian. A sign of hope and encouragement as well as of warning, declaring God to be in the midst of his people as one who defends, saves and liberates. Through the community model the Church is liberated to become a sign of the Kingdom, with the potential to become a force for the liberation of society. Although in Northern Ireland these communities are like 'a cloud in the sky no bigger than a man's hand', elsewhere they have influenced and transformed societies. Evidence of this is seen in the basic Christian communities of Latin America, Africa and Asia, to which we now give some attention.

Notes

1. *Community and Growth*, Jean Varnier: Darton Longman & Todd, p. 129.
2. *The Other Side*, Lesslie Newbiggin: British Council of Churches, pp. 23, 24.
3. *Ibid.*, pp. 15, 16.
4. *Compassion*, Nouwen/McNeil/Morrison: Darton Longman & Todd.
5. *Seeds of Contemplation*, Thomas Merton: Arthur Clarke.
6. *Ibid.*
7. *Corrymeela*, Alf McCreary: CJL, p. 9.
8. *Ibid.*, p. 9.
9. From the Covenant of the Cornerstone Community.

Chapter Five

A Church Among the Poor

Within Christian tradition there have always been communities who have found their roots among the poor, the oppressed and the marginalised. The primitive Church was composed of people whose enemies frequently described them as illiterate (Acts 4:13). In Latin America, the Philippines and parts of Africa and Asia a movement has grown up in the past thirty years that has reclaimed the tradition of the Church among the poor and oppressed. Dom Helder Camara, Archbishop of Recife in Brazil, has described it as 'the Church the people want'. It is a Church made up of countless communities of Christians 'from the same street, the same part of town or the same place of work who can come together, there we have a basic ecclesial community, a Church community'.[1] This movement has been described as 'a leaven and first fruit of an ecclesial model that is communitarian, prophetic and liberating. It is the Church at the basic level.'[2]

Basic Christian communities follow in a tradition of Christian history. The Scottish Covenanters met in secret conventicles (or basic communities) in the 17th Century. Earlier the Anabaptists, who believed the Reformation failed to deal with the social problems of power and poverty, reacted against the Reformers and quickly became subject to hostility and persecution. Congregationalism was rooted in the radical politics of its day and was instrumental in the overthrow of the monarchy. Such 'radices' – returning to the roots – led the

Calvinistic Congregationalists to face head on what many felt
to be an exploiting and unjust system. Primitive Methodism
took up the revolution, reacting against Anglican supremacy
and the deadness of official religion. The 'class' system, which
survives rather patchily today in Methodism, was at one time
a grassroots Christian movement of undeniable power and
influence. Wesley's pietism had a hard radical edge to which
his effective ministry among mining and industrial communities
bears eloquent testimony. In Britain the Quakers and in
Europe, the Moravians and the Hutterites, found strength and
resources to speak to the situation of their day as basic Christian
communities.

The Basic Ecclesial Communities of Latin America provide
us with a present-day example of the Church taking root among
the poor in the struggle for justice. It is important that we
define Basic Ecclesial Communities if we are to understand
their significance and relevance for the Church today.

The Basic Ecclesial Communities live their life among the
poor. In Latin America this refers to eighty per cent of the
population, several millions of people at the bottom of the
social pyramid. The word 'base' or 'basic' defines the status of
such people. They are 'at the bottom'. In case this should be
thought of as pejorative phrase – the word 'grassroots' is
perhaps the best English equivalent!

The poverty experienced by these people is a kind of death.
'Death due to hunger and sickness or to the repressive methods
used by those who see their privileged position endangered by
any effort to liberate the oppressed. It means physical death to
which is added cultural death, inasmuch as those in power seek
to do away with everything that gives unity and strength to the
dispossessed of this world. In this way those in power hope to
make the dispossessed an easier prey for the machinery of
oppression.'[3]

This poverty is collective. It crosses social, racial, class,
cultural and sexual groupings. The poor within base communities know how unjust structures are, and they struggle to choose

ways of freedom. The first choice is often acceptance, rather than acquiescence to poverty, a choice which has been described like this: 'We are not just a Church of the poor, but a Church which is poor in itself: one without extravagance and pomposity, without trappings and cosmetics . . . a bicycle with lots of accessories and trappings ends up by going very slowly . . . at the same time our Church ought to be humble and unpretentious, making no claim to have sole rights to the truth or on salvation . . . A poor Church, if it hasn't got chapels, meets in houses, if it hasn't got loudspeakers high up on the Church towers it will make do with some lad's guitar, a Church which, if it needs help, asks people for it.'[4]

The Spirit is bringing to birth a Church which is rooted in the milieu of exploitation and the people's struggle for liberation. People in poverty are making a choice to live in solidarity with one another and through that choice, proclaiming in life and worship, their faith in the living Lord.

The Bible is central to our understanding of poverty today. The Old Testament frequently focuses on the poor and their social alienation. The Hebrew word used most often to describe the poor is 'anawim', meaning 'the downtrodden, the humiliated and the abased'. In the New Testament the word used for the poor means 'one who cringes'. The Bible sees the hungry, homeless and those with little to wear as poor. It also sees the blind, deaf, crippled, those who are prisoners, strangers – immigrants and ethnic minorities – orphans and widows as poor. It sees those that are afflicted, depressed and hopeless as poor. The poor, in biblical terms, are those who have no opportunities or voice in society.

Justice for the poor

The main focus of the Old Testament is on justice for the poor. When we speak of justice we think of society's retaliation against the lawbreaker or of human rights. The Jews saw justice as a question of harmony, the harmonising of relationships with

God, with your neighbour and the land. Harmony with God was expressed in justice for the neighbour and in particular for the poor. The provision of land and peace to live in it were seen as a reward for acting justly (Exodus 22:21–22, Deut. 14:29, Job 29:11–20). God promised land to a rootless people, and their struggle to possess that land and live in it in peace and prosperity reveals a God who is faithful to his promise (Psalm 18:20–27, Psalm 71:14 ff and Psalm 89).

Basic Communities see poverty as something that is against God's will and God is seen as a champion of the poor. The Psalms, the expression of Jewish spirituality, reveal a catalogue of occasions where God is seen as 'a stronghold for the oppressed' (Psalm 10:9) while the wicked man is one who sets out to hurt the innocent, particularly the orphan and the widow. He is like a lion prowling to catch his prey; like an archer and a fool (Psalms 10:8, 9; 11:2; 12:5, 8; 14:1, 6).

The Psalms speak of God as committed to the relief and release of the poor and reveal a people who believe that God will save them (Psalm 10:14 following). 'Because the poor are despoiled, because the needy groan, I will now arise' says the Lord; 'I will place him in the safety for which he longs' (Psalm 12:5). God sees human life as infinitely precious, while oppressors in all ages have regarded it as expendable (Psalm 72:12 and following).

The Old Testament prophets speak for the poor. Amos, living in an age of increased material prosperity, is given the insight to see how greed was producing corruption, corruption injustice, and injustice oppression of the poor. (Amos 2:6, 7). Micah is given courage to denounce the powerful as 'haters of good and doers of evil' (Micah 3.1–4). His call to repentance and conversion is made to the rulers of the people. Jeremiah's call is for justice, the cessation of violence and exploitation of the poor (Jeremiah 22:3–5). Jeremiah tells the king, Jehoiakim, that his father, king Josiah, was one who 'dealt justly and fairly. He dispensed justice to the lowly and the poor', and he calls for his conversion to justice (Jeremiah 22:15–17).

God's law is a first call on kings who rule in his name, and they must administer it to those most in need of help (Psalm 72:1). Such words were, in all probability, spoken at a coronation. The king is to help the suffering, have pity on the needy and the poor, and exercise judgement towards those who oppress others and commit acts of violence (Psalm 72:4, 13, 14). The words become contemporary in the cries of Basic Communities calling for the conversion of those who oppress the poor. The Psalms, the Prophets and the Gospels in turn carry hope. The Messiah is the 'bringer of good news to the poor' (Luke 4:18, 19), the one who identifies with the outcast and downtrodden, with those who cringe in the presence of the powerful. He gives hope to a people struggling for change in the order of things. The Christian struggle demands a reading of the signs of the times; understanding the social, political and economic circumstances which marginalise people. This, together with the study of scriptures, will enable change to begin. This task is one which the Basic Community sees as its Christian responsibility.

Community of the poor

Basic Christian Communities are essentially cells. Together with other cells they form Churches. The Church, the 'ecclesia', is the gathering of the cells or communities. Most communities have between eight and forty adult members. By and large, communities operate most effectively with an optimum membership of thirty to forty. Basic communities do not exist in competition with the Church, but as an agent of renewal within the Church and as facilitating an answer to the question – 'What does it mean to be the Church today?'

Basic communities attract people in transition; those who do not understand God and have no theology, yet have or desire faith. They draw the weak in health, whether social, physical or psychological, and attempt to meet the needs arising from the stresses such factors put upon relationships, particularly in marriage and family life. Basic communities are not simply a crutch but provide the soil for intensifying growth and commitment.

Basic communities provide vision for the way the church's role in society can be shared; the vicar does not have to do everything! They give an opportunity for the growth of inter-personal relationships. Being larger than small groups they make for holistic pastoral planning and care; they facilitate personal spiritual renewal; from them emerge people who can lead grassroots groups and take a role in building a wider community.

Communities seek to understand their vision by being bibli-cally based, and grasping anew the apostolic emphasis on prayer and reflection. Within the community there will be experience of the theologically charged words, 'love, trust, healing, forgiveness.' Thomas Maney[5] writes of a situation in which a group responded to the needs of a family in which the father was experiencing serious medical problems. 'The neighbourhood took responsibility for the household which enabled the wife to live with her husband at the hospital. The group assumed a multitude of family duties, from chauffeuring the children and cutting the lawn to feeding the family and doing the laundry and more. In addition they secured financial help to pay for the high medical expenses. Simultaneously the whole neighbourhood came together in prayer for the father's healing and rapid recovery.'

The celebration of the Word and sacrament are central to the life of each community. Each group seeks to put into prac-tice God's word, and through the intimacy of the life lived together in cells, reveal the faith, making the mission of the Church both present and active in the locality.

Grassroots groups will not see tasks and services as their main reason for being. As groups they do not begin with an established series of objective on how to build 'Church'. The essential ingredient is human beings in search of community.

An environment of the poor – the basic Christian Community

'A Basic Ecclesial Community is an environment of Christians which can provide for the basic needs of members to live the Christian life.'[6] So how does a basic community develop? A few years ago I met Sister Maureen Grant who worked in Santiago, Chile. Her description of Chile as a beautiful country, rich in resources, traditions and crafts seemed a far cry from the images of martial law and fights between students and police shown so often on our television screens. The Mapucho people are the native tribe of Chile. Their culture is being destroyed and they are being disenfranchised by the government. Repression of peasants, tribespeople; confiscation of land which has frequently been held for centuries; and martial law have all contributed to a sense of powerlessness among the people. Working in a parish of 80,000 people, Maureen Grant was invited by some women and men, to form a group. This group sought to interpret what was going on around them in the light of the gospel. They studied Mark's gospel and as they did so, began to reflect on their work situation – for many of them, the market place. They observed that young people were at risk from poverty, unemployment and the effects of forced urbanisation upon families. As they formed themselves into communities they sought to act in the area of their concerns and resolved – 'to construct with Christ the civilisation of love'.

A sense of identity soon grew among them. At first it was expressed in simple ways with people meeting and going to Mass together. Then groups began to respond to the needs around them among people in the streets. They sought to interpret what they saw in the light of their Bible reading and reflection. Jesus became for them the pilgrim Christ who enabled them to walk in the Spirit. Sensing God's concern and desire for his people, and working on ways of meeting their needs led them to the truth that 'every experience of following brings home the fact. . . that there is no path marked out in every detail. Rather it is a way that is established in the very going'.[7] Their attitude and way of living brought a response from those among whom they lived and witnessed.

In time the group began to consider the question – 'What do you want for your area of town?' Members of the group went out into the streets and discovered the needs of the people. Three needs dominated: clean water, electric light and learning to pray. Maureen Grant accepted this experience as the leading of the Holy Spirit, a leading to which the parish responded.

Basic Communities are being formed because the people know that they must organise against increased levels of violence within the community. That violence may come from government or from terrorist sources. It may be expressed in economic or in military terms. As people unite their unity is both a protection and a preparation to work for structural change in society.

Basic communities – a response not a blueprint

Basic Communities are not formed to a blueprint. Each is a response to a particular situation. In the Philippines they flourish in a country that is eighty-five per cent Catholic and the reasons for their growth are various. One is the shortage of trained priests. Another stems from the reforms within the Roman Catholic Church which have given people greater freedom to study the Bible, to form groups and share in the Church's mission. The Bishops' Conference has given its support to the movement, although this has not always been wholehearted.

Certain characteristics can be applied to the formation and development of Basic Ecclesial Communities. These characteristics include links with the parish; small membership; trained leaders; prayer and study of the Bible together; social teaching; the use of study materials; and discovering ways of reflecting that are appropriate to the experience of the people. The communities also act as one of the means by which people are prepared for the sacraments and the task of evangelism.

In the Philippines much attention has been paid to the structure and leadership of Basic Communities once formed. Peter Batangan is responsible for training and development. When I met him in 1985 he shared with me the principles which need to be held on to by those who organise Basic Communities. For him community leaders must come from the grassroots and share a similar economic situation with other members of that community. The whole group should be committed to those who are poor, suffer deprivation and are oppressed. In addition to this leaders need to be trained, adequate material for study and reflection on their perceived situation has to be prepared. Batangan believes that study and reflection need to be done in the context of the political and social circumstances of the group. He sees the need for discussion and an analysis of the factors that make life the way it is for people. He looks for a common mind on what the social, political and economic circumstances are within the wider community. This is so that the Basic Community can agree its aims and scope of operations and choose the most effective place for work and witness.

As in all Christian experience different needs have to be met. In the Philippines three types of Basic Community function, each with a slightly different orientation. Some communities are liturgically orientated having as their primary concern the encouragement of people in regular worship, celebrations of the faith in the chapel, prayers and preparations for fiestas – a major celebration event among poor people – and Bible sharing and evangelistic work.

Others are development orientated, seeking to discuss problems and reflect on those in the light of the gospel. Each community is broken down into neighbourhood groupings of six families. Here groups of people pray, reflect on the Sunday gospel and seek to relate their conclusions to everyday life, and act appropriately. Within the wider locality particular concerns are discussed with others and, where appropriate, taken to those in authority. Each week objectives are agreed and actions planned and taken. One objective might be approaching an official over some area of concern in the community. Some would be deputed to directly intervene with the authorities, while others would pray, discuss and share with people in the wider community the plan being worked out.

Liberation communities place a high priority on education and action for justice. These groups aim for the just transformation of society. They organise, mobilise and heighten awareness among people of what are experienced as oppressive structures. Liberation Basic Communities function primarily among groups of workers, farmers, labourers, fishermen, the urban poor and national minorities.

Such a movement is dynamic, recognising that situations do not remain static. Groups may develop different emphases as need demands; a liberation orientated group recognising its weakness in worship, seeks to develop it. A liturgical group feels it is failing to deal with the issues that prevent the people being liberated from oppressive structures and begins to look for ways forward.

The Basic Ecclesial Movement is not confined to the Third World. In Europe it has made some ground particularly in Italy, Spain and Holland. In Italy the movement has been reflected in all strata of society. In the south and in Sicily where poverty is in places akin to that of the Third World, communities grow in much the same environment as in Latin America. Elsewhere relative poverty co-exists with affluence so acute adjustments are made in the lifestyle of community members. The third kind of community, frequently ecumenical, exists among the upper middle-class. One such community is St Paul's Outside the Walls in Rome whose life illustrates affluent people's capacity to make choices in favour of the poor.

This community is one in which the majority of members are in the higher echelons of academic and society life. Yet this group have chosen to identify with the poor in the city and to make one particular location their special concern. Instances

of that concern can only be illustrated here. When a local
manufacturer, an employer of considerable numbers of people,
laid off workers and closed the factory, the community of St.
Paul's gave economic, moral and physical support to those who
chose to occupy the factory. The action did not stop there, the
group precipitated discussions, raising with workers such issues
as: managing and running a factory; the nature of industry; the
moral and economic ends of industrial society – and so on.

A rich Community – for the poor

St. Paul's Outside the Walls with its substantially middle-class
community, recognises how difficult it is for middle-class people
to change their status. Solidarity with the poor becomes a
question of finding ways to identify. Those with secure jobs
concerned themselves with the closure of factories; those with
full stomachs went on hunger strikes in favour of the Third
World; those with all their physical and mental faculties
founded a committee to appeal for the Constitutional Rights
of the handicapped and invalid citizens. Those who understood
power and politics formed action groups on behalf of Nicaragua, while those whose family life was comfortable set about
forming a family life and social justice group. In worship too,
God's preference for the poor began to be acknowledged.
Many began to experience new insight into the Eucharist,
seeing it as a sign of hope for the hungry and a place of
judgement for the well-fed and prosperous.

   Basic Christian Communities challenge traditional Church
structures not only in their countries of origin but in Britain as
well. They reveal the poverty of our sense of community, our
lack of corporate commitment to the conversion of society, our
acquiescence to the status quo and above all our unwillingness
to encourage any significant movement from the grassroots.
Two reports issued by the Church of England[8] emphasise the
need for the Church to have 'a commitment to community'.[9]
One report even goes so far as to refer to a commitment to

future Church life in terms of 'Basic Christian Communities'. It sees cells existing independently of congregations, congregations being composed of cells, or congregations being self-existent and relating to a wider community of Churches, known in Anglican terms as a Deanery.

Basic Communities – not for Britain?

Faith In The City – the Report of the Archbishop's Commission on Urban Priority Areas – dismisses somewhat summarily the Basic Christian Communities of Latin America as a concept . . . 'not directly transferable to the British context'.[10] It regards such communities as 'peasant and pre-industrial, not concerned with upwards social mobility' with 'little reliance on outside professionals . . .'[11] Such a comment reveals the extent of the challenge of the Basic Christian Communities. First the comment of the report fails to acknowledge the extent of basic communities as evidenced in Italy and Holland. In such places they are decidedly not comprised exclusively of peasant or pre-industrial groupings. Secondly, the emphasis on outside professionals reveals the weakness of most programmes for Church renewal as being structural and imposed by professional clergy, business managers and synods. There is an increasing incapacity to encourage a grassroots movement within the institutional life of established Churches. 'Grassroots communities are not a new movement within the Church, they are a new way of being the Church'.[12] This is simply what the report fails to understand.

While there may be truth in the statement that Basic Christian Communities are 'not directly transferable to the British context' this is no more or less a truism than that the Book of Common Prayer was directly transferable to the 'darkest Africa' of the 19th Century! Lessons and principles from the grassroots Churches are able to be adapted and applied to the British context. We should take note of what is happening and be prepared to learn from it, so that we too can release the Spirit to create the 'Church the people want.'

Notes

1. *The Church People Want*, Document of the Diocese of Recife published by Catholic Institute for International Relations.
2. *Basic Ecclesial Community*, Jose Marino: Paulist Press.
3. *We Drink from our Own Wells*, Gustavo Gutierrez: SCM.
4. *The Church People Want*, *op. cit.*
5. *Basic Communities: A Practical Guide for Renewing Neighbourhood Churches*, Thomas Maney: Winston/Seabury Press, 1984, p. 65.
6. *Building Christian Communities*, Stephen B Clark: Ave Maria Press.
7. Gutierrez, *op. cit.*, p. 3.
8. *Faith in the City*, Church House Publication.
9. *A Strategy for the Church's Ministry*, John Tiller: CIO.
10. *Faith in the City*, *op. cit.*
11. *Ibid.*
12. *A New Way of being the Church*, Andrew Kirk: *Grassroots*, vol. 9, No. 3.

Chapter Six

The Church People Want?

In September 1983 a consultation on Basic Communities was held at Selly Oak, Birmingham. At the heart of the discussion was the desire to see what part, if any, Basic Christian Communities had in mainstream Christianity in Britain. The consultation recognised that Communities such as L'Arche, Cornerstone, Iona and many others[1] reflected an intention towards the poor, but it agreed that Base Ecclesial Communities as such did not exist as a grassroots movement in the United Kingdom.

The consultation concluded that there were various reasons for this. A number of factors that worked against the formation of Basic Communities were given as follows:

- A lack of solidarity among poor and marginal people.
- An over-dependence on inadequate state benefits.
- An unwillingness by many to enter into conflict with authority to obtain justice.
- A preference among the clergy and lay people for a traditional approach to religious faith and practice.
- An over-emphasis on personal religion coupled with an inadequate understanding of what it means to share together in religious life.
- An historical lack of lay leadership.
- The insistence that the traditional role of women is maintained.

- A lack of education and understanding on what it means to be the Church today.
- An inadequate understanding by people on how to reflect on their personal spiritual experience and in particular how to relate to scriptural teaching on justice and peace.
- A lack of biblical knowledge. People sense scholarship and their understanding are too far removed.
- The Bible is read from 'above' rather than 'below'. This is revealed in a tendency to spiritualise the manifesto of Jesus (Luke 4:16–20) and the Beatitudes (Luke 6:20f). The gospels are not read and understood from the standpoint of their being written, by marginal men among a marginal people.
- A misunderstanding of Basic Christian Communities, seeing them (like the House Church movement) as a threat to the institutional Church, rather than a means of giving it life.
- A recognition and acknowledgement that the building of trust takes time.

Since the consultation met political, social, religious and economic changes have taken place. These may create an environment in which Basic Communities can form. These changes include increased unemployment; some evidence of willingness to enter into conflict to obtain justice; a further decline in traditional religion; and reports from many denominations on the need to develop new patterns of ministry. Within society, and increasingly within the Churches, a movement resisting the traditional role of women is gathering strength. The decline of union power, the increased repressiveness of legislation, increasing police and military power all contribute to the need to discover 'a new way of being the Church'.

In order to look realistically at Basic Christian Communities as an option for Churches in the UK, we need to face some of the obstacles and objections that have been presented.

A lack of solidarity among poor and marginal people

There is little doubt that a lack of solidarity among marginal people is a basic obstacle to the formation of such Communities in the areas described by *Faith in the City* as urban priority areas.[2]

'Solidarity is the key word of the international labour movement . . . It means standing shoulder to shoulder, struggling together, suffering for one another, and living with one another in a single community.'[3] It is a word and concept which lacks power in the UK situation.

In his *Making of the Working Class* E P Thompson wrote, 'From 1816 onwards working men were putting themselves into a new stance in relation to other social groups and were developing new solidarities . . . it is partly a question of morale. At its simplest level it meant that it was possible for individual working men to have a sense of sustained commitment to a movement for their own class objectives, and a confidence that enabled them to stand up against the physical and moral resources of their opponents.'[4] Solidarity is essentially about resisting the rule of the few over the many.

In his major study, *Poverty in the Inner City*,[5] Paul Harrison has given an insight into marginalisation and powerlessness in the eighties. It is a disturbing report, revealing a lack of solidarity among people who live in urban priority areas. A staggering twenty to forty per cent of the population of the UK live in urban priority areas. Of this figure, some twenty per cent fall below the list of private basic needs drawn up by the International Labour Office for developing countries, which include:

- enough food to maintain health and work capacity
- sufficient clothing to avoid social stigma and personal shame
- adequate heating and insulation to prevent excessive cold and damp

- basic furnishings and floor coverings
- a tolerable home for each household.

Harrison argues that if to this the following list of social needs were added, providing for a basic minimum standard of living within the UK, the remaining twenty per cent would be included:

- education and training permitting full participation in society and in the economy
- preventative and curative health care
- full and equal access to the law
- adequate support in disablement and old age
- effective family planning
- sufficient play and leisure facilities for the young within reach of the home
- transport to work and leisure without excessive cost or inconvenience
- freedom to walk the street without fear
- the right to participate fully, at work, in the neighbourhood and in local services, in deciding on matters that affect one's life.

These limited needs are in one way or another unavailable to significant numbers of people in urban priority areas. 'No secret police, no written law, no overt repression, no explicit arrangements cause this state of affairs. It is simply the result of a tendency observed in almost all human societies without the strongest safeguards and common values to prevent it: political power and economic power go hand in hand. And the converse: economic weakness results in political weakness which in turn prevents effective measures being taken to alleviate economic weakness'.[6]

What has happened to the solidarity which Thompson so confidently spoke of as being at the heart of the working class movements of the 19th Century? Many factors which contributed to this can be listed: wars, particularly the First World War with its accompanying loss of idealism, and manpower; recessions, leading to the slumps of the pre-second war era; the subsequent post-war slumps, booms, and further recession. An increase of social mobility; immigration; the break-up of the extended family; urbanisation and the dismantling of intimate communities, re-housing of population in isolated environments; the innate conservatism of trade unionism; the fluctuation of the benefits of the welfare state according to the political preference of the government in power can also be added. Socialist movements in the UK have failed to galvanise marginal people and win their allegiance, largely because of self-interest and a desire for power, rather than solidarity. This has resulted simply in failure to stand alongside brothers and sisters in their need.

The institutional Church has contributed little to marginal groups, siding as it so frequently has done in history with the establishment and the status quo. A working man of the early 19th Century quoted by E P Thompson[7] said, 'The working classes are gathering knowledge, and the more they gather, the wider becomes the breach between them and the different sects. It is not because they are ignorant of the Bible. I revere the Bible myself . . . and when I look into it . . . I find the prophets stood between the oppressor and the oppressed, and denounced the wrong doer . . . however rich and powerful . . . When the preachers go back to the old book, I for one will go back to hear them . . . but not until then.'

The biggest single factor that has limited the impact of the solidarity Thompson predicted, is the slow decline in consciousness of just how bad things are, by those among the working-class comfortably enough off to live outside the ghettos. Jeremy Seabrook in his *Landscapes of Poverty* makes this point powerfully. 'When the poor attack each other, fire the ghettos, mutilate others and damage themselves with drugs or alcohol, it has this advantage to the rich, that the connection between them and the poor has been so effectively shrouded that they cannot be accused of complicity in the damage that is done to the poor. The poor can be safely left to demonstrate to the world their instability and violence; and to show that they are poor because they deserve nothing more; while the wealthy proceed, serene and inviolable in the enjoyment of their just deserts, going about their business and only dimly aware of the red glow in the night sky, barely perturbed by the sirens of the ambulances that fetch out their freight of torn and wounded humanity from the impenetrable ghettos. The rich have been delivered from the consequences of their own actions; and it is perhaps only to be expected that this absolution leads to a certain jubilation, an assertiveness which they had, for a brief levelling interlude after 1945, forborne to parade. After all, the poor ask nothing more than to be able to imitate them; no longer to expropriate, let alone abolish them.'[8]

Socialism in the UK has lost touch with those really at the bottom of the pile. Derek Hatton, Ken Livingstone and Tony Benn may have got much of the practice wrong, but what they touched is the relentless sense of injustice and exploitation felt by many people. Solidarity is missing for and among the poor.

'Is solidarity – the word and the concept – another expression for the Christian way of life, and for the motives behind Christian action? Is neighbourly love the Christian term for solidarity? Is solidarity the socialist word for neighbourly love?'[9] If it is, then the Church has more common ground than it normally perceives in sharing its gospel with the poor.

We need to ask in what ways are people isolated from one another? How do people get divided, separated, treated and paid differently? What criteria are used for differences of treatment? The principle of divide and rule dominates our society today. 'Everyone becomes his own best friend. Fear of losing jobs, and therefore their living, isolates people.'[10] This can be seen by the events within the National Union of Mineworkers during the Spring of 1984 when a significant group within the Union refused to strike, thereby preventing the strike from becoming effective. At the heart of the issue was the fact that oppressed mineworkers themselves became the oppressors.

The hope of being able to save oneself by sacrificing another is always the means by which solidarity is destroyed. As Moltmann comments, 'There is only one way of protecting every single one of us: solidarity with the first victims, solidarity with the weakest among us. What affects them today will affect us tomorrow. So their skins are our own.'[11]

Solidarity has to do with resisting tyranny, oppression in whatever form whether it is intentional or un intentional. It has to do with liberating oppressed people, promoting consciously the human and equal rights of all. That is always Christian, even if it is also socialist.

Solidarity is to do with entering into the suffering of others, the guilty and those who can no longer help themselves.

'Compassion, sharing another person's guilt, grieving with him and standing by him when he is dying demands a solidarity that goes beyond activism and the illusion that there is something to be done *about everything*. It demands a fellowship in impotence, in helplessness and even in silence'.[12]

Solidarity is about being in community. Natural communities 'follow the precept birds of a feather flock together'.[13] Homogenous communities – whites, blacks, Christian, Jews – frequently are communities that reflect only an 'insatiable need for self corroboration'. We need people who share our opinions and are on our own wavelength.

Jesus built community on the principle of hope. In such a community 'people who are dissimilar are united, develop a vital interest in one another, and become similar through their creative love'. 'There is neither Jew nor Gentile, male nor female, bond nor free . . .' and one could add, educated or uneducated, employed or unemployed. 'No, they all become one in Jesus the Messiah, and joint heirs of the promise of the future' (Galatians 3:28f).[14] A solidarity of love heals the wounds of a divided society, breaking through into acceptance and hope. Basic Communities could help that to happen.

An overdependence on inadequate state benefits and an unwillingness by many to enter into conflict

Many who have little need of the welfare state cannot see that there is anything wrong with it and believe its handouts and benefits to be the answer to all social ills. Others see it as the means by which 'scroungers', 'ne'er do wells', and the 'work-shy' are enabled to thrive. In reality, inadequate state benefits with their attendant red-tape and humiliating procedures, leave many permanently poor and deeply needy within society. People in most need do not know how to fight to achieve their rights. Even if they did they would be unwilling to enter into the necessary conflict for fear of losing the little they have.

'Welfare benefits are typical of the "rights" that the citizen enjoys in Britain. They are not guaranteed rights, there is no one to ensure that everyone automatically gets what they are entitled to. There are no loudspeaker vans touring the streets broadcasting their existence; no itinerant social security officers knocking doors to check no one is forgotten. The benefits exist, but people are left to their own devices to find out about them and apply for them. Many stumble on them by chance. Many pass them by unknowing.'[15] The problem of the social security system is that it is a system without checks and balances. Many who are dependent on state benefits are inarticulate and ill-informed. They face a bureaucracy that fears paying too much to the wrong people and is geared towards its own protection. A young trainee DHSS employee quoted by Harrison was endeavouring to point out the benefits available to a would-be claimant and was told by a supervisor – 'That's not our business. You should answer only the questions that are put to you. We don't want any more on our workload.' Such an attitude springs from the burden of overwork, an inexperienced and rapidly changing clerical staff, together with the sheer pressure of demand from clients.

From within my own parish I have seen what happens when an articulate, educated middle class individual takes up the

cause of someone who for weeks has been fobbed off with
inadequate benefit, and answers fed by the machinery of
bureaucratic confusion. The recipient, having an advocate,
received all of his entitlements, but he would never have done
so left to his own devices. Even so, by no standards is he well
off.

The response of people to the injustice perpetrated by the
system is the response of the powerless: it is either anger,
leading to violence, scrounging, a black economy; or
submission and depression, with its attendant isolation, fear,
and manipulation. Basic Communities in other situations
develop from just this sense of injustice, solidarity is their
hallmark, confrontation with authority to obtain justice their
direction.

Historically the institutional Church has rarely responded to
the kind of situation produced by overdependence and unwillingness to enter into conflict. However, *Faith in the City* has
set clear agenda for the Church and the nation to tackle this
and other issues. While seeking to co-operate with the government, the Church is beginning to recognise that it may well
have to confront the government and face the attendant consequences. Whether or not those who worship in our Churches
will welcome such activity remains to be seen. Most people still
prefer a traditional approach to religion and religious life, and
this becomes a limiting factor in itself.

Personal religion and shared faith

Since the Enlightenment, Western Protestantism and Catholicism have tended to see Christian faith as being essentially
about personal matters. It is about 'my relationship with God'.
Sin and salvation are personal concerns. The experience of
Basic Communities is that 'sin and salvation, while affecting
the individual person, are understood more in corporate and
structural terms. Conversion is a process. The community of

faith is constantly 'being converted' to God in Christ through the Church, to the Word and through the neighbour'.[16]

The concept of Basic Communities as we have seen is not foreign to Protestantism. Yet, 'most Protestant Churches today appear to be more concerned about maintaining a dubious respectability even in the face of institutionalised injustice and violence, than in speaking out in defence of fundamental human freedoms.'[17]

Too much British Church concern focuses around our apparent 'religious liberty' – our freedom to preach the gospel. Such freedom can take precedence over other freedoms. The freedom to have the basic needs of food, shelter and clothing was primary to Jesus' understanding of the gospel. (Matthew 25). When other freedoms are denied in order that the gospel may be preached it too becomes oppressor, and its true practice prevented. Christianity in the West is essentially middle class. It has given little attention to its own contribution to the creation of poverty and urban priority areas. 'The combination of our private preferences and the ramifications of our political choices are returned to us as . . . an unequal society.'[18]

Our dependence on personal religion and piety is reflected in the way in which Church buildings have become the focus of our religious activity. Maintenance of Church plant, clergy stipends and the paraphernalia of worship patterns, form the mainstay of Church business meetings. *Faith in the City* recognises the burden that buildings and plant so often are, but still fundamentally perceives the Church as comprised of buildings which are the centre of its religious activity. As we have seen, Base Communities do not.

As far as sin and salvation are concerned, our emphasis upon the individual, and the Basic Community emphasis upon the corporate and structural, raise a number of salient questions. Once we recognise that conditions of poverty and oppression are not 'given', can we refuse to enter into the struggle to change things? Does our doctrine of personal sin deal in any way with the question of institutional sin? We give weight to sin as a transgression against God, but do we give as much concern to sin as transgression against neighbour? Do we who have traditionally understood humanity as 'lost' have any words of comfort for those whose lostness before God relates to their feelings of inner loneliness and alienation from people? These are important questions for they prise open our over-personalised view of sin and salvation.

Within both the Western and the Third World Church 'folk religion' plays a significant part in the lives of people. Despite years of argument and counter-argument 'four wheeled religion' – the pram, the wedding car and the hearse – are still the dominant expressions of that folk religion. Basic Communities in Latin America have grown up in an environment dominated by these and other forms of folk religion including Spiritism. In seeking to come to terms with nominal Christian association Basic Communities have sought to re-evangelise the people with a fresh message of salvation through Jesus Christ. To do this within a peasant, pre-industrial situation a denunciation of the demonic elements in Spiritism has been necessary. Superstitions carry power to further marginalise people, so their denunciation is seen as a pre-requisite for the formation of a Christian community reflecting the Kingdom of God. Jesus recognises the need for this too (Matthew 9:34, John 7:20, John 8:49.) In developed, industrial and even post-industrial societies the more sophisticated elements of demonic influence expressed in Materialism need similarly to be denounced. Only by this kind of denunciation will folk religion cease to be fundamentally superstitious and become a base for true evangelism.

Evangelicals have placed great emphasis on personal conversion, as a pre-requisite for membership of the Church and the Kingdom. For many that conversion process is deemed to be complete at the moment of commitment. Such conversion marks the point of repentance – at least in theory – where 'turning to God from idols . . . from darkness to light, from the power of Satan to God' takes place.[19] Such an emphasis is not so clear in Third World situations. Conversion there is perceived as a process. The whole person in his whole environment undergoes a continuous process of conversion. This means being converted from idols, spiritual and material; places of security and power, prejudice and fear. We in the Western church need to grasp this perception of conversion if we are to be free from idols, prejudice, fear, misplaced security and power. So often what passes for conversion amongst us is seen by others as little more than enlightened self-interest in terms of the world to come.

This chapter portrays the Church and society at large as uncaring, and lacking in a corporate will to see things change for the most needy within our country. Solidarity, 'neighbourly love', mutual responsibility, are lost in self-interest and self-protection. Individualism is endemic, and in the end, it is 'my best interest' that matters. At the bottom of the social ladder, a scramble for the bottom rung becomes unseemly, ugly and violent. Those who look on, feel that while there is confusion underneath, at least their own position is a little more secure. Upward social mobility is still the order of the day and nowhere is this more evident than in middle class Christianity.

Leadership structures within the Church contribute much to the malaise. The expectation upon the clergy to be 'jack of all trades' means that they are seen as the hub around which all things in the Church revolve. This is often reflected in an attitude that says 'This is our Church' when things are going well. But when things are going badly, membership drops, and the question is put to the Bishop or Vicar – 'What are you going to do about it?' Methodism in its earliest development encouraged participation in 'clashes'. These were lay-led, a significant 'grassroots' movement. Lay leadership was paramount within other non-conformist groupings and still is formally although in practice it has waned. Lay leadership has always been lacking in episcopal Churches – Anglican and Roman Catholic. What is needed is a re-generation of responsible lay mission within the Church. Base Communities could provide this.

Notes

1. L'Arche works among mentally handicapped people, and has community houses in France, Britain and throughout the world.
   Cornerstone is in Belfast; Iona has communities in Iona and Glasgow.
2. *Faith in the City*, *op. cit.*
3. *Power and the Powerless*, J. Moltmann: SCM, p. 105.
4. *The Making of the Working Class*, E P Thompson: Penguin.
5. *Inside the Inner City*, Paul Harrison: Penguin.
6. *Ibid.*, p. 135.
7. E P Thompson, *op. cit.*
8. *Landscapes of Poverty*, Jeremy Seabrook: Basil Blackwell, p. 96.
9. Moltmann, *op. cit.*
10. *Ibid.*
11. *Ibid.*
12. *Ibid.*
13. *Ibid.*
14. *Ibid.*
15. Harrison, *op. cit.*, p. 140.
16. *Basic Ecclesiastical Communities* A Study of Re-evangelisation and Growth in the Brazilian Catholic Church, A. William Cook Jn: International Bulletin of Mission Research, July 1980.
17. *Op. cit.*, p. 144.
18. *Faith in the City*, *op. cit.*

Chapter Seven

The Professional Church?

In recent years renewal movements within the Church have recognised the growing need for a ministry of the laity. The growth of pastoring schemes in Churches has given rise to 'Lay Pastors', 'Elders', 'Pastoral Visitors', 'Street Wardens' and so on. By and large these are understood as assistants to the 'Chief Pastor' – the Vicar or Minister of a Church. Such people are rarely seen as the generating or motivating influence in contemporary Church life. For the most part clergy are the hub of the Christian community and lay people are content, or at least compliant with this situation. Grassroots Communities have begun to understand and express the truth that Jesus and his gospel, rather than clericalism and structures, lie at the heart of the Christian community.

As has been said, the Church has neglected lay leadership. Non-conformity has elevated its Elders and Deacons to officials and Church bureaucrats, while Anglicanism has formalised lay ministries and placed them squarely on the side of the clergy. Class divisions have also made for clerical dominance, particularly in working class situations where the patronising and condescending attitude of clergy towards their congregations has been little short of scandalous. While priests and theologians are seen as integral to the whole life of the Christian community there is little doubt in the minds of liberation theologians such as Gutierrez that 'theology can no longer be done as work during the day, but it must be done as reflection at the end of the working day'.[1] The work or unemployment of the day, must be the stuff of theology – our search for understanding God – so that people are enabled to reflect on what it means to be the people of God. Priests, Ministers and theologians must increasingly be those who enable people to interpret what they are experiencing in everyday life in terms of the gospel of Christ.

The past thirty years have witnessed the development of synodical government in all the mainstream denominations. This apparent growth of democracy has been all but surpassed by its attendant bureaucracy. Theoretically lay people have a greater say in the government of the Church. The suspicion exists, however, that little has changed, except perhaps that the pace of change is even slower now as such lengthy consultation has to take place! What has not changed is that synods and congregations have not 'felt the weight, the pain and pleasure of actual responsibility . . .'[2] Responsibility for the Church in the locality is still fundamentally clerical and clerics continue to dominate congregations and make decisions for them.

Grassroots Communities have learnt to bear the pain and pleasure and the weight of responsibility for the Christian body. They have learned to use clergy and religious (nuns and monks and those in lay orders) as guides and spiritual resources, rather than general practitioners or managers. For clergy in the UK to become resources of spirituality, guidance and support, rather than uncertain, ill-trained managers of congregations calls for new procedures of selection and training.

The Basic Communities are structured organisms of faith, hope and love animated by Jesus Christ's message of fraternity, liberation and communal participation. They exist as signs among us of God's Kingdom. In their life and witness they anticipate and prepare for the Kingdom of God and God's coming people. Their existence challenges hierarchies which they see as having monopolised sacred power.

Communities look to hierarchy to put its own house in order.

They perceive God's Church as servant rather than a self-perpetuating, self-authenticating authority, holding power on its own say so. Hierarchy must be seen as a mediator for justice within and for the wider community. In this role it must ensure that the structures which monopolise and marginalise people are dismantled, including where appropriate its own. If it has a role as co-ordinator, that role must be in co-ordinating the activities of peoples, structures and policies already enabling mediation for justice.

Tensions do exist between Base Communities and the established Church structures. This is because there is 'a Church of lay people on the one hand and a Church managed and led exclusively by clerics on the other . . .'. What is needed are 'more balanced relationships, which allow for greater participation by all in producing and enjoying religious goods'.[3] This tension between Base Communities and the institutional Church needs to be recognised. It is an important one. Nevertheless such tensions do not necessarily mean threat; creative tension can be the very means by which life is given.

Hierarchical structures are crippling the Church. The maintenance of structures is costing ordinary people dear. Quotas, the sums of money raised in Churches towards maintenance of ministry, are increasing alarmingly every year. For the most part they are imposed. Thus, as has happened recently in one Diocese in the Church of England, parishes are simply 'refusing to pay' saying 'we will give what we can afford'. Often such action produces 'penal measures' against dissenting groups. What is happening is far more significant than just withdrawal or refusal to pay money. Maintenance of the structure is simply seen as 'not worth it'. New models become imperative.

Since Constantine the Church has been there for everyone. With its recognition by the state and its receipt of state authority the Church lost its visible form of community. Civic affairs and Church affairs became synonymous. Parishes and Dioceses were structured around political regions and districts. Priests became officials of the state and the Church. Their authority increased, and their office became authoritarian. In England the Rector was the lord and master of the parish.

The Enlightenment, with its subsequent effect of privatising religion, marked the beginning of an identity crisis for the Church. The institutionalism and growing privatisation of religion has emphasised the lack of a visible form of community. The power of Church in state has of course been curtailed and yet this has given rise to many questions. 'What is the Church in our world today? Is it a religious copy of society? Or is it Christ's witness for society? Is it something that separates people from one another? Or something that builds community?'[4]

The historical division of the Church into clergy and laity; and the changing nature of Church membership once the Church became acceptable, has created a Church 'from above' coming into being. 'Community in the Church was replaced by community with the Church . . . the Church which takes care of the people, but in which the people themselves have no say. This is the Church's hierarchy, as "holy rule", but not the gathered congregation, the assembled people of God.'[5]

Professionalism is a major feature of European Christianity. In Germany for instance, clergy are paid by the State as civil servants. When people witness change in the Church they witness it as change from above. Such change is seen as structural. The professionalism of the clergy must be safeguarded. Their role justified. In an increasingly professional world however, the question must be asked; 'What is the distinctive professional nature of the role of clergy?' Because congregations are essentially passive, the very means by which the established Church operates, the Church is trapped in a model that makes it a Church for, rather than of, the people. 'If all Christians were active members, this Church for the people would cease to exist and a new Church of the people would come into being. But this is not what the organisers and theologians of the established Church want.'[6]

Much ecumenical development in recent years has led to the

idea that through team ministries, pastoral centres, specialised ministries, para-Church organisations, a sort of nationwide spiritual security net will be produced. Such a Church has been described as 'the service Church'.

Clerical professionalism and lay passivity have ruled out the possibility of a 'ministry of the whole Church'. Faith being essentially a private affair, is typified by the children's chorus 'You in your small corner and I in mine'. Religion is played at, opted into or out of at will. Charlie Schultz in his classic cartoon has one of his Peanuts characters declaring 'I love mankind, it's people I can't stand'. Great play is made upon the concept of love, in the Church of today. It is love for mankind in general, but for no one in particular. Jesus did not teach about love like that. 'He dealt with each individual person who came into his life or into his thoughts, in such a way that nobody was ever excluded and everyone was loved for his own sake and not for the sake of his ancestry, race, nationality, class, family connections, intelligence, achievement or any other quality. In this concrete, personal sense Jesus loved all men and lived in solidarity with all mankind.'[7]

People have an inadequate understanding of how to reflect on personal spiritual experience. This has come about because of our excessive individualism. Spirituality is about 'knowing God'. It is lacking in our Church today because it involves discipline and in that discipline attentive listening. The heart of spirituality is simplicity. It is not about having complex jargon-technique. It is about knowing and believing God. Jesus spoke very simply. He talked in pictures, in terms that people could both identify with and make their own. He used the illustration of 'everyday things'. He said few words, but those he said, he said often. He wanted people to 'perceive God', to know him and believe him. Such belief calls for knowledge upon which to lean the whole weight of belief. Knowledge 'of', is not the same as knowledge 'about'. To have knowledge of God is to seek to know him in all the dimensions of our life and being. To know him in such a way that everything else – status, reputation, possessions – are of no consequence. This spirit is not abroad in the spirituality of the Church. Where it is present it creates a harmony of will – out of such harmony comes activity in solidarity. Spirituality is about imitation of God – Christian spirituality, 'the imitation of Christ'. Individualism comes about because there is within 'institutionalised religion an institutionalised absence of commitment'.[8] A religion that demands nothing, and offers nothing.

Insistence that the traditional role of women is maintained

It is part of the nature of a religion that demands nothing and offers little, that it should hold on to such authority as it has by continuing to marginalise women both in ministry and hierarchy. It is recognised that no theological reasons exist whereby women in Episcopal Churches (Anglican and Roman Catholic) should not be priested. The reasons given for failure to act are in terms of expediency and timing. These are the devices of the powerful against the powerless. They reflect the trivialising of sexism. Women have a capacity for intuition that is rarely perceived in men. It is an un-nerving experience for many because so often a woman will get to the source of a situation more completely than a man. Man is jealous and fearful of woman. She can give life and birth within her own being, a disturbing and profound mystery. Her very nature is touched with earthiness, keeping her in the rhythm of nature in a way man can never know. Fear governs so much of what we do not know. Fear governs the reason of man in not giving to woman her rightful place in the ministry of God's people. Fear roots in prejudice, prejudice in legislation, legislation in oppression. We oppress what we cannot understand, wonder at, or appreciate.

Women within the Latin American Church taking 'Jesus as the starting point (have realised that) the behaviour of Jesus towards women is consistent with his mission and message of justice. The imitation and following of Jesus. . . . entails the obligation to get beyond the cultural and ideological obstacles that oppress and marginalise women'.[9]

Within the Western Church there have been cosmetic attempts to recognise women's distinctive contribution to salvation history but the oppression of women, which has existed under all socio-economic systems, has continued. 'Capitalism gives women a role in the family, and it used the family to reproduce and maintain itself as a system of domination.'[10] This includes responsibility for daily restoring of the bread winner; producing children, preferably sons, as the labour of the future; encouraging submission to the system; developing and channelling consumer potential, all in the service of the capital. The effect of this is to lead to a set of social conditionings that significantly oppress women.

In the Church, a significantly patriarchal institution, women rarely participate in decision making. The structure being hierarchical and masculine, 'is a model of the oppressive man-woman relationship. At the level of conscience and faith the male dictates what a woman is supposed to believe and practise'.[11]

Elizabeth Moltmann-Wendel argues that Jesus sought to break down the traditional patriarchal nature of religion, but as Christianity developed patriarchalism once again dominated religious thinking and practice. She says. 'We Christians can no longer ignore the fact that women were the only ones who did not flee when Jesus was taken captive. It is the women who are recognised as the actual bearers of the tradition of Jesus' death and resurrection, the early charismatically organised congregations reflect this privileged status of women, much to the amazement of their environment. Women could lead congregations and were apostles and bishops . . . In the person and history of Jesus, the traditional animosity toward women was suspended. In fact he himself personally integrated so many male and female behavioural characteristics that one could consider him the first maturely integrated person.'[12]

From the Latin American experience the Church is learning that while woman is present in the Church *en mass*, she is absent from the direction and management of the Church. Women have resolved that if 'liberation theology is to mature . . . the rule to make every effort to incorporate elements specifically rooted in the situation of women into any and all theological articulations'[13] must be made. Such an idea needs to re-echo across the Church in the West.

In their conclusions on the 'Role of the Latin American Woman', the Mexican organisation 'Women for Dialogue' stated, 'For a theology based on the reality of women, we think it is important to remember that the incarnation of God's Son took place in the humanity of the poor, and that his resurrection is the victory of the new humanity over death. It is the dynamics of a God who became poor first and foremost, rather than male or female, and who overcomes death to create a new humanity devoid of divisions by class, race or sex (Galatians 3:28)'.[14]

In a sense the experience of Latin American women reveals something still uncomfortably true about Western feminism. Feminism as we know it concentrates on promoting equal pay an opportunities for women. However this movement is notably among a small section of women who aspire to the high status male professions. By and large feminism has not touched the working class of the West, and black and Third World women do not identify with the Western feminist movement, believing it does not tackle the problems of economic, cultural sexist oppression. Elizabeth Wendel sees the need in the Western Church for a response to this, and argues, 'the sub-culture must be uncovered and listened to as the alternative to the dominating culture. This need applies to the scholarly world as well as to our present Christian culture, which is still so strongly patriarchal. Engaging in this task means letting fantasy have a legitimate place alongside dogmatics, experience alongside our written heritage. It means a rediscovery of the Holy Spirit not only as dogma but in practice. In concrete terms it means recognising that women have the right to speak, to let their imaginations be felt, and to share responsibility in the Churches and in theology.'[15]

The priesting of women in episcopal Churches is long overdue. It is an injustice that needs to be righted forthwith. However, women need to recognise that they will be entering an existing hierarchy. Despite the alternative perspective they will bring to things, it will not be enough to have simply entered a former male bastion of privilege and status and sit in the leather armchairs. Women, to make *their* priesthood valid, must not only bring a feminine perspective, but work towards the de-hierarchicalisation of the priesthood.

Equally women in the Western Church must recognise and repent of their failure to perceive the reality of the struggle for those women who recognise that 'the incarnation of God's Son took place in the humanity of the poor . . . it is the dynamics of God who became poor first and foremost, rather than male or female'. Gaining access to the power structures should not be seen as an end in itself. Access, once achieved, must be spent in re-structuring those structures in a truly incarnational way. The incarnation always means being down among people, events and circumstances, and moving towards an alternative humanity where 'life is hid with Christ in God'.

Individualism – the most important religion?

Lack of solidarity, overdependence on inadequate state benefits and sexism are all reflections of individualism which has been described as 'the most important religion in Western industrialised countries'.[16] Individualism militates against the deep human need to belong, be loved and be needed. When 'having' becomes more important than 'being' the 'others' lose their value and community is destroyed. The inner city riots across Euope are the reactions of those whom Jesus called the last – the unemployed, uneducated, uncared for, futureless people. Their cry is that they become 'the first'.

What is called for among us is a spirituality that rejects

individualism and reflects community. This spirituality must refuse to believe 'things have always been like this', and go on to believe things can be different, and that we can make them different. Jesus refused to resign himself to things as they were. Such a choice of the heart demands sacrifice. Today we must make such choices. 'Spiritual life can only be a revolutionary life.'[17]

If seventy per cent[18] have some notional belief in God, the Christian task is to understand what keeps it notional. Is it that Christians are seen as unconcerned or ambivalent about the things that cause resignation and a disbelief in the future? The environment, the Bomb, militarism, individualism and sexism are seen by many Christians as topics of debate, rather than powers and principalities to be resisted. The process of turning the world upside down engaged in by the early disciples grew from a tradition that dared to interfere with the powers that be. That daring brought hope and commitment to many.

Our inadequate understanding of what it means to be the Church today, our incapacity to reflect on our spiritual experience in the light of scriptural insights on justice and peace, leave many of us wallowing in a faith that has to do with 'my God and my spiritual life', rather than a life lived in community and resistance against 'the world, the flesh and the devil'.

Notes

1. 'Towards a Church of the People', Robin Greenwood: *Theology*, Nov. 1983.
2. *Op. cit.*, p. 423.
3. 'Theological Characteristics of a Grassroots Church', Leonardo Boff: *Challenge of Basic Christian Communities*, Orbis, pp. 134–135.
4. *Power and the Powerless*, J Moltmann: SCM, pp. 159, 160.
5. *Ibid.*, pp. 159, 160.
6. *Ibid.*, p. 159.
7. Jesus before Christianity, Albert Nolan: SCM, p. 59.
8. Moltmann, *op. cit.*, p. 163.
9. *The Latin American Woman*, Praxis and Theology of Liberation, Cora Ferro, *op. cit.*, p. 35.
10. *Ibid.*, p. 26.
11. *Ibid.*, p. 28.
12. *Humanity in God*, Elizabeth Moltmann-Wendel: SCM, p. 38.
13. *Ibid.*
14. Ferro, *op. cit.*, p. 35.
15. Wendel, *op. cit.*, p. 50.
16. *Doing Theology in a Divided World*, Orbis.
17. *Ibid.*
18. Statistics given in *Faith in the City*, *op. cit.*

Chapter Eight

A Different Church

It is hard to be different. Most of us do not like to make choices that put us out of step with things as they are. Part of the reason for this lies in the way we have been brought up within the Western world to be dependent. We are dependent upon the state for our welfare and protection; upon jobs and family life for security; upon the institutions of government, education and the Church for telling us what to do and how to do it. Choice, for the most part, is limited to decisions within the existing order of things rather than against the existing order of things.

In the situations where Grassroots Communities have grown up choices have to be made that are essentially outside the existing order. In Ulster movement towards reconciliation began when ordinary people faced a situation they found intolerable and a system which was devoid of hope. They chose to act together for the sake of others. Similarly, Dom Helder Camara saw the Church people wanted as springing from choices that no longer accepted poverty, prejudice and oppression as the way things had to be.

Within our Church and society many things are intolerable and yet they are accepted as the way things have to be. Within this so-called acceptance lies much that is negative, critical and destructive. Dependence in Church or state makes the criticism of others easy and self-criticism difficult. It is easy to be negative, critical and destructive. It is much more difficult to choose a path of resistance, challenging the powers and principalities that dominate our lives and call for conformity. Any dependent society makes criticism of 'them' easy and self-criticism of 'us' difficult. Situations that demand reconciliation call first and foremost for a willingness to be reconciled within ourselves. When we face ourselves and the structures of which we are a part critically, acknowledging our unwillingness to change, we have in our power the process of repentance. It was this repentance that formed the cornerstone of the process of change set in order by John the Baptist and Jesus.

Jesus saw resistance to all that prevented the rule of God being established, as an integral part of repentance and discipleship. His resistance to authorities that refused to acknowledge the sovereign power of God, whether in the Jewish religion, the state or society, led ultimately to his execution at Calvary. The choice that Jesus faced and presented was both stark and costly (Luke 9:22–25). Jesus presented people with a challenge; the power to change things existed within and among themselves. Christian people have failed to apply this in our day. We refuse to accept that God's intention for us is that we live to the full potential of our humanity. Living to such a potential is acknowledging that under God we have the freedom to think, choose, act and take the consequences of our actions. While in no way wanting to deny the representative nature of the death of Jesus, it came about as a direct consequence of the choices Jesus made in his life. Choices about the way he healed, fed, criticised, encouraged, gave hope to, and pronounced judgements against people. His actions grew out of his prayer and intimacy with God, and was worked out in and through an often inadequate community of disciples.

For the majority of people, even those who are most committed, the Church is in some way there to 'meet needs'. Because of its history of paternalism the clergy are expected to be on hand fulfilling whatever needs are demanded of them. People feel that the Church is primarily there to take care of them. This is what it means to be dependent.

The task of the Church is to disciple people in such a way that the Kingdom of God is established. Pastorally its energies should relate to that task. By and large the Church has failed to meet the expectations its parish structures have encouraged. This should hardly be surprising. Clerical control of the Church has prevented real 'power from below' being established to change things. Such control has led to unreal expectations of pastoral care. Pastoral care schemes have been developed in many Churches, but their very development reveals among people a sense of having second best. In my own parish when a lay-pastor scheme was introduced, at least initially people felt that such care was a substitute for 'the real thing'. In reality people in my parish are more cared for now than at any time in the past. Clergy by and large choose a select few people from an overwhelming number, the few becoming their special concern.

Little evidence exists in the English Church of the desire to exercise power from below. The relative stability of political systems of the West has encouraged a Church membership that reflects the prevailing dependency of society. Dwindling numbers and influence, restructuring of ecclesial areas, diminishing manpower in clerical terms have not been sufficiently devastating events in themselves to create the environment necessary for change. Though many experience a sense of impending cataclysm and apocalypse, there is still sufficient ambivalence to prevent change.

The cataclysm of Northern Ireland provided a significant tool for sharpening the mind. Attitudes in both commmunities have hardened, and there is a real danger that the worst is yet to come. For those who have seen cataclysm as a place from which reconciliation must eventually come the difficult path of repentance has begun, and everything has had to be re-examined. At the heart of charge is a process of relearning.

Learning for change

The relearning process began among Grassroots Communities;
when misunderstandings, naked prejudice and misconceptions
were faced, dialogue started. Confrontation formed the basis
for new relationships of trust and support to develop. For the
most part relationships do not play a major part in our Church
life. People do not have to get on with one another in Church.
They can always move further away to an empty pew; move
to another clique; or leave for a different Church or no church
at all. For the most part we do not have to face personal or
idealogical disagreements. Religion among us being essentially
a private affair, how I worship God is my business and how
you worship him is yours. Much of what is done in Church on
Sundays could be done on one's own. Any Vicar who has to
listen to a catalogue of complaints Sunday by Sunday knows
only too well the place of private worship! The distractions that
prevent us worshipping God – 'I was distracted by the children.'
After an experiment with greeting one another at the Peace –
'I don't come here to look at or talk to people in the Holy
Communion of all services!' After some new songs in worship
– 'Do we have to have music that a parrot could learn in 30
seconds?' Attempts at discussion of a teaching point in a sermon
would in most Churches be tantamount to calling for a walkout!

Such reactions are understandable. Our modern world is
a confused and confusing one. Among White Anglo-Saxon
Protestants (WASPS) the world is highly competitive, individualistic and lonely. Religion is not experienced as a communal
activity, bearing consequences for how life is lived elsewhere.
Because it is a private activity, carried out with little understanding or participation, it simply becomes a place of refuge.

People live their lives in different spheres and relate to the
world through the opportunities and problems that each of
those situations presents. The problems and opportunities of
the neighbourhood are different from those of the work base.
Clubs, societies, Church, all produce different matters to be

experienced and resolved. In each of these situations there is a measure of security and seduction. The situation which offers most security and advancement obtains the highest priority of commitment, while everything else takes second place. Hence the low priority of the Church, in most people's lives. When the external world of full employment, quiet neighbourhood, and secure family life are blown apart by some cataclysm then the order of priorities changes – and alternatives have to be found. But not until then!

Most Christians face a conflict between their religious experience and the way they have to live life in the everyday world. It is often the way the Christian faith was taught that produces this conflict. In the world of business, commerce and industry, decisions are made on the basis of being right. While new systems, structures and practices may come into an insurance company or manufacturing industry, the fundamental skills of knowing how to see a good risk or make a good product continue to exist. Being right is seen as the means by which action is validated in our world.

It is this 'needing to be right' that John Hull[1] sees as a major problem for Christian adults in terms of learning the faith. 'The need to be right carries with it the fear of being wrong. In the lives of may Christian adults these factors prevent learning. To be ready to learn is to be ready to admit there is much that one does not know, that one may not be entirely right. There is even the risk that one may be proved wrong.'[2]

It is true too, that there is a hidden if not explicit belief that being Christian is about having a basic corpus of knowledge before your faith can be lived out. Many Evangelicals talk about the need for 'more teaching', but whether in fact it is 'more learning' and 'different ways of learning' that are needed is an open question. The learning of Christianity is essentially that of relationships – understanding who we are in relation to one another and to God – rather than the amount of head knowledge we have of our faith. Although, I hasten to add, this is not a plea for lazy thinking or oversimplifying what is profound and mysterious.

Obviously in this life there is much that we do not know; much we will not know; and much we cannot know. In the discipline of being adult in the secular world, we recognise that everything is in a process of change. Such change demands continual adaptation. Adults face new situations and overcome problems through study, enquiry, questioning, forming hypotheses and being willing to change their way of thinking. Having changed we plan and take action. The process of good upbringing in childhood has to do with equipping children to take responsibility for themselves and their actions. It is this taking of responsibility that is missing within the Church.

What happens to most adults in Church is that they are returning to childhood – if not infancy – in the processes of dependency. 'One goes to Church just as one goes to Hospital as a patient, not as an agent, to be acted upon and not to act. One is preached at, one receives Communion, one is helped, one is led in prayer, one is refreshed. Even where some learning takes place, the passive expression continues. One is instructed . . . The congregation is the ground upon which the seed is cast, it is the little flock which is led by the shepherd, it is the vine which is pruned. Responsibility lies with the sower, the shepherd, the vine dresser . . .'.[3]

Discovering how to take responsibility forms the substance of answering the question 'What does it mean to be the Church today?' To take responsibility means facing the twin possibilities of success and failure, learning to experiment with ideas, programmes, new ways of doing things, renewing of relationships and taking the consequences of the risks involved. A paradox is presented to us in the teaching of Jesus. He sees the place for forward and careful planning, but he also recognises that there is a certain risk in putting the hand to the plough – and not forever looking back to what might have been (Luke 9:62)!

Worship is having good dreams

Worship and learning are priority areas for making choices. A friend of mine says that 'worship is the shop window of the Church'. I think he is right – at least at the moment. The necessity for worship to be 'of the people' rather than 'for the people' is a first priority. If worship or liturgy is 'the work of the people' then ways have to be found to make it so.

There are some signs of this happening. The whole development of folk arts in worship, with the recognition that musicians, artists, dramatists, actors, poets and dancers have something to give to the whole experience of worship is important. The community at Taizé with its emphasis on simplicity in music and chants, the use of light and colour, and the encouragement of pilgrimage to discuss and work at reconciliation, peace, and unity have given worship expression to the grassroots young.

Worship demands imagination, the freeing of the spirit within those who participate, so that they may find a place where God is raised up in the midst of his people. The limitations of tradition in worship need questioning. We must recognise that a sense of God is not automatically conferred by the speaking of many words, singing of many hymns, the lighting of many candles or the breaking of much bread at the Communion. It is what people bring of themselves to these things that gives them life. We need to see light, colour, music, dance, poetry, prose and prayer as gifts we bring to the act of worship.

I belong to a Church where we feel some excitement about our worship and we certainly put a lot of effort into preparing it. Yet it is still essentially imposed rather than emergent. I have a deep resistance to things that are 'shoddy', and also to worship being perceived as something that 'if only we are open to the Lord' will happen among us. There is a world of difference between 'leaving it to the Lord', and groups of people sensing together their gift in dance, drama, reading or prayer and making that offering available to the act of worship in which we all join.

Within the Anglican tradition of the Church considerable emphasis is placed upon the liturgy which forms the base of its worship structure. Rarely are these structures seen as tools to be used, picked up or put down at the need of a worshipping people. More often they provide an excuse to continue in inflexibility. There is a wealth of liturgy hidden within the experience of God's people. Our Church environments rarely reveal it. We need to free all that experience in our worship. Liturgy springs out of a sense of history and a sense of belonging. The cycle of human experience is composed of conception, pregnancy, birth, marriage, death, celebration, hope, fear, tragedy, war, peace, plenty, poverty, harmony, disunity and much else besides. So often, the only way these things are brought into our worship experience is when someone leads the prayers. Then it is all too often stylised and frequently inadequate.

Grief may seem an odd experience on which to build a liturgy, but in the history of our congregation in this past year twelve people have died. Is their passing just a matter of history, or is it also a part of our present? What does it say about us as a Church? Are those people really missed among us? Has our understanding of grief and bereavement been deepened because of their passing? Has the quality of our life been changed by their death? Has it given us a place of solidarity with those whose death is more tragic, more public, less dignified? In our worship tears are rarely shared, yet they are a common gift enabling us to identify with others in sorrow and joy. Bereavement is not just experienced in dying, but in leaving. How much do we understand this in relation to our marriages and family life? What does it mean for the church to truly live as the people of God? What impact should events of our life have on liturgy?

In recent weeks our local Taizé group has gone on small pilgrimages to places of discomfort, pain and suffering in the

London suburbs. Through simple acts of worship, discussion and prayer, attempts are made to understand the effects on people of experiencing unemployment, sexism, racism and other aspects of powerlessness and distress. Within such an atmosphere worship becomes more than token solidarity, it becomes a place of identity. Such pilgrimages reveal a vital way for the Church to be active in its locality. They are an opportunity to express publicly our faith and solidarity with the people around us. Liturgy becomes truly 'the work of the people'; witness becomes an act of standing alongside, and revealing the truth of God's concern to redeem both circumstances and people. Such worship is not only celebratory and compassionate, but at times also an expression of judgement.

As worship and liturgy grow from the story, the history and experience of congregations, so that which is offered to God and to one another will become all-embracing. Birth, childhood, marriage and death are rites of passage that recur in the experience of congregations. Within the liturgy of life the cadences of grief, loneliness, sickness, death, sadness, and loss have their own place in the story of a people. All these things provide rich resources for the language and participation that worship demands. No one is excluded, all have something to offer and to share. We simply have to find the means by which that can happen.

What happens among us as congregations is a microcosm of what happens in the wider world. State of being, for instance, is often overlooked in both life and worship. The single, by choice or circumstance, as well as the one parent family or the widow; the orphan or the little ones and those whose sexual orientation differ from the norm: all have their place in worship. We should question the extent to which state of being is reflected in the language and activity of our worship; the need for language to be inclusive rather than exclusive – using words like 'all' instead of 'men'. Many women find the use of men-only language deeply offensive. Conflicts and places of disagreement need to be acknowledged within the framework of our worship. The issues that fragment our world break us up as congregations too. The issues of racism, sexism, affluence, poverty, hunger, unemployment, violence and war. We have got used to disguising them rather than facing them. A liturgy and worship that is of the people, will be one that faces the pain of division as well as the unity of celebration.

Such a shop window of worship would provide the basis for the mission of God's people. Within the existing framework of worship of God's people lies the instrument for such expression. The instrument is the Eucharist – known variously as the Holy Communion, the Lord's Supper and the Mass. In choosing to use the phrase 'the Eucharist', I do not mean to imply any particular bias. At the root of that word is 'thanksgiving', and at the heart of the prayer of all Christian tradition is thanksgiving for the life, death and resurrection of our Lord Jesus Christ, and the benefits won for humanity by his death on the cross.

Eucharist – the feast of imitation and discipleship

The Eucharist is the way in which the disciples of Jesus continue to demonstrate their choice and desire for things to be different. 'To be imitators of Christ' (1 Corinthians 11:1).

Such a choice, writes Joseph Grassi[4], is 'at the very core of the Eucharist (and) is a solemn pledge or covenant to be a disciple of Jesus, to imitate his lifestyle. This brings the Eucharist into the practical sphere of everyday life. This connection between the Eucharist and discipleship is found within the meaning of Baptism. While Baptism is the first initiation into Christian life, the Eucharist is the continued renewal of this commitment.' Paul reminds us that those who are baptised into Christ are clothed with him. 'All you who have been baptised into Christ have clothed yourselves with him. There does not exist among you Jew or Greek, slave or freeman, male or female. All are one in Christ Jesus' (Galations 3:27,28). Such an act of clothing is by its nature an act of identification and imitation. This verse reminds us that through baptism people who are clothed in Christ oppose those things that separate and segregate individuals and groups. Racial barriers, sexual equality, class barriers are all broken down. When we partake in the Eucharist we pledge ourselves to imitate Jesus and go on breaking those barriers.

The Eucharist is the feast of the imitation of Christ. St Paul was not afraid to recognise the place of both example and imitation as aspects of Christian life and behaviour. The baptised believers are invited by St Paul and the community who lived and worked with him 'to make more and more progress in the kind of life you are meant to live; the life that God wants, as you learnt from us and are already living it' (1 Thessalonians 4:1 JB). Do our acts of celebrating the Eucharist contain within them a sufficient sense of calling to those who participate? Does our celebration of the Eucharist inspire us to live in ways that imitate the life of Christ? I fear all too often not.

One significant reason lies in our tendency to 'spiritualise' the act of breaking bread rather than to experience it as part of our day by day encounter with other people. Paul saw this danger. In his often quoted and misunderstood passage in 1 Corinthians he tells the believers that their celebration of the Eucharist is 'not profitable but harmful' (1 Corinthians 11:7). It is so, because poor and hungry members of the community are embarrassed by the way the comfortable and well-fed ignore their situation (1 Corinthians 11.17–22). Paul wants people 'to discern the body' recognising that 'worship without justice is a sham and insult to a God of justice'.[5]

The commandment of Jesus 'do this in remembrance of me' is central to the Eucharist. As a young Christian I found Holy Communion confusing and frankly boring. I sat in the Baptist Church where I developed as a Christian, and listened to the solemn words tacked on to the end of what was frequently an already overlong occasion. In due solemnity I tried to picture the feast, the garden, the betrayal and the cross – we seldom acknowledged the resurrection at this service. One Deacon 'gave thanks' for the bread and another for the cup. Try as I might, evocation, nostalgia, emotional recollection all failed to work. I frequently left feeling confused and empty. Once I began to see the Eucharist as a place where discipleship and a continued willingness to imitate Jesus were pledged publicly, a new sense of 'remembering' came into being. I discovered the truth that 'in eating broken bread, was the Christian pledge to become like Jesus; to assimilate his lifestyle and to obey his word'.[6]

Eucharist bread for the hungry

More recently I have become aware of the need for the Eucharist to be earthed in the reality of the world as it is. Such a world, as in Jesus' time, is hungry and thirsty as well as satisfied and full. If the assimilation of Christ's lifestyle is fundamental to the Eucharist, then the concern of Jesus for the hungry must also be integral to the Eucharist. Jesus saw the hungry, thirsty, naked, homeless and imprisoned as part of himself. Matthew 25 illustrates this in its account of the judgement of God. Those who are finally accepted as Kingdom people are those who have fed the hungry and so on. In this action Jesus says he is fed – 'I was hungry and you gave me food'.

Jesus acknowledged the need to see prayer for daily bread as integral to Christian action and lifestyle. For those of us with plenty, such a prayer gets spiritualised – food for the soul is what we pray for. While the bank balance or the promise of a pay cheque lingers, while our supermarkets store plenty, such a prayer will never touch the depths of conviction that a tenacious starving Ethiopian will give to it. While millions starve the Eucharist celebrated among the rich becomes an act of judgement. If it does not lead to concern expressed in action, action which ultimately leads to an end to hunger, then our celebration is simply not rooted in discipleship and obedience to Jesus Christ.

At its simplest the Eucharist is an act of sharing. 'The simple central action of the Eucharist is the sharing of food – not only eating but sharing.' This act of sharing was first done by Jesus, not with his family but his disciples. By this act of sharing bread and wine he created an effective symbol of every man and woman living as brother and sister, sharing the earth's resources. In the Eucharist Christians are called to covenant together as a community to continue the ministry of Christ to the poor.

Our action at the Eucharist is not to be seen as a private 'my communion' but as 'our communion' for the sake of others. Paul understood the intimacy of the discipleship meal, seeing it as a process by which people become 'one body'. 'The fact that there is only one loaf means that, although there are many of us, we form a single body because we all have a share in this one loaf' (1 Corinthians 10:17 JB). Such a closeness and commitment produces a solidarity of relationships. 'If one part is hurt, all parts are hurt with it. If one part is given special honour, all parts enjoy it.'

The Eucharist is a central act of sharing, remembrance, discipleship and imitation. It is the sacramental expression of giving. Other forms of giving are seen as flowing from that act. The giving of money is seen as a weekly discipline (1 Corinthians 16:1), sharing our plenty with those who have little (2 Corinthians 8.13–14), but the Eucharist speaks of something more than just the giving of money. It calls us to find ways of 'making connections between the Eucharist, the bread of life, and food for the hungry'.[7]

The work of the people

Making connections is essentially practical. I'm grateful to the work of Joseph Grassi in helping us to make those connections, and his ideas are freely quoted in this section. Our Churches need to establish 'hunger committees' in order that we might keep hunger as an urgent priority. The first task of such a group should be to educate and inform, looking for practical ways of connecting 'the Lord's Table with the table of the hungry both locally and internationally'. Secondly, such a group would look at ways of consciousness-raising over hunger issues and related problems. Churches would have liturgies of hunger at penitential seasons such as Advent and Lent. Prayers, readings, sermons and even the liturgy of the Eucharist itself could be reshaped towards the poor.

Liturgy being the 'work of the people' – actions should spring from it. Projects for the hungry and needy could be set up. Newspaper articles and television programmes highlighting hunger could provide the basis for a resource centre equipped with letter-writing materials, addresses of relevant government agencies and their offices of state. The attention of politicians and others could then be constantly drawn to the poor.

Workshops and hunger related events like soup dinners and 'rich man poor man lunches' can be ways of keeping the hungry before us. Sooner or later, however, the Church needs to find concrete ways of experiencing what it is to be hungry.

'Painful hunger is a daily occurrence that must be counted by an ongoing effective programme that enters into the lives of every Christian . . .' One such way is to rediscover fasting as a part of both individual and corporate spiritual discipline, learning how to do without the things that have become necessities for us.

We know that Jesus experienced what it was to be hungry and poor and that much of his ministry was serving the needs of the hungry and the oppressed. 'He came to bring change in the political, economic, and social structure of First Century Palestine. The Eucharist is the renewal of the covenantal relationship Christians have with Jesus. It is a renewal of our pledge of discipleship to him. To be a disciple of Christ means to imitate him – it means to struggle for structural change in our societies and to be obedient to the Father, the God of justice.'[8]

Worship is essentially an act of resistance. It resists the idea that humanity is in control (or out of control) of its own destiny. It resists too the pervading sense of powerlessness – that nothing can be changed. It bears witness to the sovereignty of God in all things. It reminds us particularly in the Eucharist, that all true worship involves a cost, a sacrifice, a laying down of rights, status, privilege – so that God's authority and power may be revealed.

Worship is an act of obedience, and as such is not passive but the result of a decision, a choice. The choice which Joshua laid before the refugees from Egypt was this: 'Choose you this day whom you will serve . . . I will serve the Lord' (Joshua 24:15).

Such a choice results in a commitment to struggle; wrestling against apathy, lukewarmness and a sense that things are impossible. It is a choice to cease being disobedient. Worship is revealed as a profoundly political act because it raises the question of who God is for us in this world; the extent of our love for him, and our willingness to serve him against all other gods.

In the Latin American Basic Christian Communities people have learned to combine worship and political struggle. In the light of a growing sense of powerlessness in the West we must learn to do the same.

Notes

1. *What Prevents Christian Adults from Learning*, John Hull: SCM, p. 91.
2. *Ibid.*, p. 141.
3. *Ibid.*, p. 142.
4. *Broken Bread Broken Bodies*, Joseph A Grassi: Orbis, pp. 82–92.
5. *Ibid.*
6. *Ibid.*
7. *Ibid.*
8. *Ibid.*

Chapter Nine

A Resistant Church

Resistance is the common experience of all innovators of
change. If we wish change, we must expect resistance; if we
would change we must resist. The place of tradition, if not
history, is close to the heart of many within the institutional
structures of the Church and the state. Historical bases for
tradition are rarely accurately recalled or remembered, nevertheless traditions are held on to strongly. Tradition whether in
terms of Church practice, human rights, freedom, worship or
whatever else is a complex historical mixture of religion, economics, culture and politics.

The late 18th Century saw the emergence of Christianity as
an essentially private and pietistic affair. In the West it exists
essentially in that form today. It was not always so. Thus the
'tradition' that Christian practice is individual and between 'me
and my God' does not have deep roots in history. If we go
back to the time of Constantine we can see his conversation as
a direct political consequence of the sense of threat an emergent
Christianity posed to an internally weakened Roman empire.
Christianity was no 'hole in the corner' but was regarded as a
serious alternative society. If, as Lesslie Newbiggin has
reminded us, 'the Church had been content to regard itself as
a society for the promotion of the personal salvation of its
members. . . it would have enjoyed the protection of the law
– the same protection which judges enjoy in modern culture,

available for the same reason – namely that they pose no threat to the ideology which controls public life.'[1]

To understand the nature of the resistant Church we need to look briefly at its history. The impact of Constantine's conversion – whether spurious or genuine – was to make thinkable what was previously unthinkable – namely 'the world had become Christian'. While considerable misgivings were felt by many 'the experiment of a Christian political order had to be made'.[2] Within that political order anti-Semitism quickly emerged. By 380AD orders for the violent suppression of Judaism and heresy were given. As the experiment turned into a system so the pre-Reformation Church in Europe became all powerful, monarchical and despotic, holding over all the power of life and death. The Crusaders, whose warriors symbolised the Christian world view, sought to annihilate and subdue Islam. The medieval Church united religion, government and culture across Europe. With the Reformation and Counter-Reformation and the setting up of state Churches the uniformity of medieval Europe began to be fragmented. Nationhood and the primacy of the nation-state soon emerged. The Church-state tie-up was essential for power and control.

Resistance to the power of the state and the Church soon appeared. Puritanism in Britain led to the revolution of the 17th Century, the outcome of which was the right of Christians to worship as they chose and the ability to form communities to worship in. Resistance in Europe was marked by both Anabaptists and Roman Catholics. In Ireland freedom of worship for Catholics came much later and Cromwell, champion of Puritanism and the freedom to worship, is regarded as the single greatest suppressor of Irish Catholicism. The foundation of the United States grew from the desire for freedom to worship in the manner of people's choosing. The plethora of sects emanating from the United States today is testimony to the continuance of this historical tradition.

While Puritanism may have led to the revolution in Britain and the subsequent rights to freedom of worship, it is the influence of the Enlightenment with its accompanying humanism that made effective such rights. From the time of the Reformation Europe prospered. Integral to that prosperity was the growth of urban communities. These communities grew up as a result of trade and the emergence of rich middle-class merchants. Their commercial interests and travels raised them above the religious and political divides of Protestants and Catholic, Church and state, and their crossing of national boundaries gave them a broad world view. The humanism of the Enlightenment brought a tolerance and in time, respect for the individual. Human rights grew both in state and Church.

The privatisation of faith

The privatisation and individualisation of faith had its roots in the Reformation. Luther, whose rediscovery of Paul's teaching on justification by faith has formed the cornerstone of Protestant theology for over four hundred years, saw that 'decision for faith in God . . . is always a decision against the devil'. This decision lies at the heart of all conflict both individual and corporate. This conflict is continually present and represents a tension between contradicting God and conforming to God. Luther saw this tension and conflict existing until Jesus comes to bring in the Kingdom. Such a division produces 'conflict in the world and in the life of every single person. Because God and faithful beings correspond to each other, human beings in faith contradict the godless world and the world contradicts them and leads them into trials and suffering'.[3]

From this position Luther formulated his doctrine of the two Kingdoms – a worldly kingdom and a spiritual kingdom. This view has influenced Christian thought concerning the Kingdom of God ever since. 'In the worldly kingdom law, good works, reason, the punishing sword, and rewards for good deeds are valid. In the spiritual kingdom only grace, justification and faith are valid. In the worldly kingdom the sword rules, in the spiritual kingdom the Word rules. In the spiritual kingdom God provides eternal salvation. In the worldly kingdom human beings must care for the temporal welfare.'[4]

What Luther sought to teach was that 'the world is not and never will become the Kingdom of God; rather it is a good earthly order against evil chaos. One should deal spiritually – which means with faith – with God and his gospel. The gospel does not create a new world but saves people through faith'.[5]

The doctrine of the two kingdoms has caused Christianity real difficulties. Where do Christians place their allegiance? Do they ever act politically? And if so, in what ways? Are they effectively bound in a trap that must serve God *and* mammon? Luther's doctrine created the climate for individualism and pietism. 'The world was left to unfaith, and faith returned into the introspection of a pious soul . . .'[6] God-consciousness had nothing to do with the world of politics and humanity.

The effect of Luther's two kingdom thinking led, in the 19th Century, to both the privatisation of faith and the legitimising of the state as 'a law unto itself'. In due time Church and state became effectively divided, the Church able to 'bless' but not 'dialogue'. Thus all sorts of social manipulation, wars and the unchecked growth of capitalism, became legitimate and beyond the influence of the Church. It either had to bless or bite its tongue. Ironically it was in Luther's Germany that Hitler exploited the two kingdoms argument irrevocably. In a disintegrating post-First World War society, Fascism promised economic recovery in return for authoritarian rule. Order and law became the means by which disruptive elements, Jews, Communists, Liberals and their attendant philosophies could be suppressed. 'Within this full separation of the two kingdoms, the gospel of the kingdom of Christ was made impotent on the one hand and on the other the right of arbitrariness was given over to the existing powers.'[7]

Individualising of faith has led to the failure of the Church to be a force for resistance – except in individual and local circumstances – against racism, expressed in its most horrific form in the European holocaust; against militarism and the dominance of the bomb in human affairs; against sexism, still regarded as irrelevant by most Christians; against the evils of poverty and exploitation revealed in the various manifestations of communism and capitalism.

The history of the Church is the history of humanity. Throughout its story there have been 'moments of grace and abject sinfulness . . . times of prophetic witness and shameful betrayal'.[8] In the present period of history the Church throughout the world is recognising its weakness and its place with those who are powerless. A shift in emphasis can be discerned. It is a shift towards seeing everything as a whole, and of seeing God as intimately concerned with that whole and its salvation. Salvation is not split between two kingdoms, it is for the whole world. 'If Christianity is to regain its messianic power, it must overcome the situation of privatisation. As a private matter it cannot be a messianic matter.'[9]

Let me introduce a personal note here, despite this chapter's emphasis on the corporate as opposed to the individual. The writer of this book is male, white anglo-saxon and Protestant, middle class, married and heterosexual. He is a citizen of a capitalist country which is a member of an affluent economic community, and a political and military alliance which threatens the very future of humankind. Those facts in themselves are enough to make him, in many people's eyes, one of the oppressors of this world. Clearly to try, as an individual, to carry responsibility for that fact would result in madness, despair, or suicide. Yet as Christian people together, as a Church, we need to learn to take responsibility for who we are in the light of the gospel of Christ, and discover ways of transforming the world.

The challenge to me, then, is – 'What will be my practice in this context?' or rather, 'our practice,' for I cannot imagine a true practice that could remain individual. We know with Marx that, 'We are not about the business of explaining the world, but transforming it.'[10]

Choosing to resist by listening

I was born in the closing stages of World War II. My father, who fought in it, was deeply touched and angered by Belsen concentration camp which he entered shortly after its liberation. The holocaust was the subject of many conversations with him. For me, intuitively rather than inductively, it exposed the power of oppression whether in race, sex, class, economics or militarism. The impact upon me as a child of twelve watching Montgomery's account of the liberation of the death camps was a deep shock, profound fear and an overwhelming sense of helplessness. A couple of years later, 'I gave my life to the Lord', and realise now that was, at least in part, an interiorisation of God, Jesus and everything else. Unable to cope with the horror of the world as I saw it, I sought refuge in a religion that was essentially private and pietistic.

People of my generation find it hard to reflect on the horrific events of over forty years ago. We do not know how to respond to the Nazi holocaust, Hiroshima and Nagasaki. Part of the difficulty is one of history, the other of geography and anthropology – they happened 'a long way away' and 'to other people'. Yet those events exposed the viciousness of racism and militarism. They exposed too the conflict of ideologies, capitalist, communist or fascist, and the resulting oppression of not only the conquered but also the conquerors.

In our generation the machinery of racism, militarism and genocide is evident in the evils of apartheid in South Africa; the famine of Ethiopia; the military and right-wing dictatorships of Central and Southern America. The true impact of the struggle for Nicaragua to free itself from either Western or Eastern domination has not been fully realised. All these things, if not long ago, seem far away. Within our own United Kingdom the conflict in Ireland and the bloody violence of Brixton, Tottenham and Handsworth are neither long ago or far away. What evidence exists that Christians have seriously sought to engage as a Church with the powers that lie behind such manifestations of oppression and violence?

When people dominate in race, culture and class it is easy to believe that all is well – even in the face of the most appalling evidence to the contrary. J B Metz, the German theologian, in reflecting on Auschwitz said 'unfathomable. . . is the silence of men: the silence of all those who looked on or looked away and thereby handed this people over to an unutterable loneliness'.[11] It is, I am sure, no way forward to postulate what many have wanted to saddle contemporary Germans with, namely some kind of 'collective guilt'. Yet we do need to have a moral awareness of the past. 'We can only mourn history and win from it standards for our own actions when we neither deny the defeats present within it nor gloss over its catastrophes'.[12] Being aware of history means being able to live our lives in an awareness of what has happened not an evasion of it. 'It also means that there is at least one authority that we should never reject or despise – the authority of those who suffer.'[13]

We make a great deal of being a multi-racial, multi-cultural egalitarian society. Many people in that society feel they are victims. Blacks and Asians recall enslavement and colonisation; they see citizenship given in order to be of use to a society whose own natives in increasing numbers refuse the menial tasks that mark the transition from an industrial to a post-industrial society. We need to recognise those who suffer, the victims of an exploited racism by a so-called Christian nation.

Much these days is made of the word dialogue. It is seen as a bridge between alienated groups of people. At a recent meeting one of my white fellow clergy was feeling sore that he was the victim of what he termed 'black racism'. He was surprised that he could not 'dialogue' over a particular issue. He felt it was unfair. He was being openhanded – and fair. He had forgotten, as had most of us present, that victims are not allowed to speak. Dialogue can only begin when we have learned to listen to what people are saying about themselves, rather than telling them what we want to say about ourselves in relation to their sense of grievance. Do we really know why young blacks have espoused Rastafarianism? South Africa's blacks and Latin America's poor, a theology of liberation? Do we know what the Jews believe and why? Or the Buddhist, Mohammedan or Hindu? Do we care? Or do we simply feel frightened and overwhelmed at the possibility that our own securities and the poverty of our faith in Christ will be exposed?

I listened recently to one of the leaders of the new right in English Evangelicalism. Under the guise of exposition of the Scriptures he preached against Islam, Hinduism and other forms of what he called syncretism in our country. He warned of an Islamic intent to convert London by the year 2000 AD. He didn't ask the question – even if the premise was true – as to why? Such an approach underlies the incipient racism that lies at the heart of Christian behaviour. We are apathetic and insensitive to those who are deeply wounded, who are angry and rebel against the religion of the conqueror – our 'Christ the King'. Should we not feel judged rather that in Jewish-Christian-Moslem dialogue, a 'Shiite Moslem with his tradition of the Sovereign God, felt the lack of God's self-surrender to man, the God who suffers and sacrifices himself'?[14]

Choosing to resist in repentance

Part of our incapacity to be sensitive and compassionate to the suffering of others stems from our understanding of Jesus as Messiah and of the end times – the Day of the Lord. Both Jews and Christians believe in the Messiah. Jews cannot accept Jesus Christ as 'the chosen one'. Christians can and do. Both perceive that the Messiah is to be a reconciler, judge, restorer and redeemer. Christians believe that reconciliation begins in the here and now. Such a belief has been interiorised so that it has to do primarily with personal redemption. The sense of being O.K. with God has left much Christian witness apathetic and insensitive to the catastrophe and disasters of the world.

Both Christians and Jews believe in 'the Day of the Lord'.

Such a belief gives voice to a deeply held conviction that one day there must be a vindication, a judgement upon all that is happening and has happened. For Christians the Day of the Lord is all too often perceived as a time of triumph, a kind of grand clearing up job, in which God will right all wrongs and dish out appropriate punishments to the baddies – none of whom will be Christians – who will get crowns and well-dones all around! For Christians this life contains a 'foretaste of glory divine'. What is all too clear, even if over-parodied, is that our perception of Christian reconciliation takes little account of reconciliation, justice and working for the establishment of peace – all prerequisites to the Day of the Lord.

The Old Testament prophets, by and large, warned against anticipating the Day of the Lord. 'Woe to you who long for the day of the Lord. Why do you long for the day of the Lord? That day will be darkness not light' (Amos 5:18). Other prophets also speak of unspeakable suffering and judgement as integral to the day of the Lord (Joel 1:15, Zechariah 4:19ff and Micah 5). The context in which such a day is looked forward to is one of repentance, expressed in resistance to seduction and the living in, and hoping for, justice. In these terms the Day of the Lord can be anticipated with joy as the day when the rule of justice and peace becomes available to all (Micah 4.1–5). Can Christians look forward in hope without first having something 'to wait and fear . . . not just for themselves but rather for the world and for history as a whole?'[15]

For Jews, and others who perceive themselves as victims of oppression, the 'Day of the Lord' must be one in which they are seen as vindicated. Persecuted peoples gain a capacity for resistance. Jews have maintained a nonconformity and identity as a community despite the very worst; blacks have formulated their own defence and resistance. Most Western Christians have become political conformists, hiding the heart of their faith in untouchable spirituality that has lost its practical expression. Racism and oppression in all their forms highlight the need for a Christian practice that recognises that discipleship of Jesus is political. 'It is mystical and political at the same time, and it leads us to a responsibility for not only what we do and fail to do, but also for what we allow to happen to others in our presence and before our eyes.'[16]

Choosing to resist in community

The creation of groups of people who will become communities of resistance in our generation is of paramount importance for the Church. Failure to engage in this task will reflect an unconscious resignation to the existing disorder. We need to acknowledge that our faith has kept us from any significant encounter with reality. It has been a comfortable but unbelievable faith. It has been a faith lacking in immediacy, compassion, questioning and sensitivity. Concerned about being 'right' we have frequently got it 'wrong'. It has been a faith that has refused to set up a significant climate of resistance in which God can act in human affairs. 'God's grace is the ability to resist in time – and constantly.'

The communities of resistance that have grown up within Ireland, Latin America, the Philippines, Italy and elsewhere have done so in countries where capitalism, liberalism and 'Christian', that is to say anti-communist, ideologies have dominated government. They have grown up among the very people who are victims of capitalism and liberalism, the poor, the powerless and the deprived. Yet for many Christians throughout the world there is no conflict in accepting Christianity as instinctively identifying with capitalism and the Western understanding of democracy.

Within the kind of Christianity developing among Basic Communities different influences have affected the practice and development of faith. These influences have included Marxist thought and a Marxist understanding of social, political and economic structures. The main influences have come from Church leaders who have seen the reality of poverty, oppression and marginalisation in their own countries. These men and women have then reflected biblically on what they have seen and experienced, and concluded that the structures that have shaped national life for many centuries are inadequate and wrong. They see the poor as victim, and their oppression as victimisation. From these perceptions have grown what we know as the theology of liberation.

In the West there is a deep fear of Marxism. Western nations, particularly the United States and Britain, have supported highly repressive regimes in Latin America, Asia and Africa because their leaders – whatever their other faults – were at least anti-communist. Such paranoia has been expressed by the United States over the Sandinista government in Nicaragua. Every effort, politically, military and economically is being used to try to bring down the Sandinistas.

In the 16th Century Luther rightly argued that the Christian faith is not the property of any political or social system. It transcends structures and cultures. Luther in his time saw this as meaning that there was no need any longer to be bound by medieval structures and cultures. When the Sandinista revolution occurred in Nicaragua, Christians but particularly evangelical ones 'had to discover painfully, that the gospel was not inseparable from the United States allied Samoza dynasty, that is now yesterday's nightmare. Too many Nicaraguan evangelicals made the mistake of believing that God would never allow a staunch anti-communist 'Christian' like Anastaso Samoza to fall. Now they know how wrong they were'.[17]

The Reformers recognised that a gospel rediscovered, purged of its medieval adornments and distortions, could co-exist with the emerging society. Nicaraguan Christians are recognising within 'the highly organised social and economic experiment occurring in this land' a similar capacity for a rediscovered gospel, purged of its capitalist and liberal adornments. In my meeting with Gustavo Parajon (a Baptist Pastor and President of the Evangelical Committee for Aid and Development – CEPAD) I found a man, initially fearful of the Sandinista government, who could say after five years that he did not fear it any more. 'Our greatest fear right now is from the United States government and the threat it is to *our* revolution.'

Choosing to resist liberalism

Miguel D'Escoto is a Maryknoll priest and sometime Foreign Minister of Nicaragua. He sees the government of Nicaragua as being formed through the influence of both Scripture and Marxist thought. His reflections are symptomatic of the influence the Basic Christian Communities are having throughout Latin America and Asia. Most Western Christians cannot perceive how Marxism can be used as a tool for social analysis that can benefit the gospel or the Church. Liberalism is seen as the traditional ally of Christianity. Such a position is anathema to people like D'Escoto and Parajon. D'Escoto once said 'there has never been anything more diametrically opposed to Christianity than liberal philosophy'.

Liberalism is about encouraging selfishness in humanity. If people are to work and produce they must be appealed to at the level of their selfishness. To do anything else is idealistic and unrealistic. Such selfishness means that human beings are doomed to suffering. Many have to be exploited in order that some can have what they want. Exploitation is of resources as well as people. The growing ecological crisis is directly attributable to unchecked exploitation of land and fossil fuels, pollution of water, nuclear power and so on. Movements like the Ecology Party, Peace and women's movements are in part a resistance to this unchecked rape of humanity and its resources – a universal dimension of liberalism, reflected in different forms from Manchester to Managua.

Liberalism denies the wholeness of the person. People are split into parts or activities. 'Today is Sunday. I must therefore be religious. Tomorrow I will be about making money, doing politics and so on. The business of business is business.' Just wages, justice for the poor, safety for the handicapped are not primary concerns for business and government in capitalist societies. Profit is the all-consuming concern. Capitalism becomes the economic expression of liberalism. People must be made to work, and the most effective incentive is material wealth. 'The poor cannot be freed from the cruel visitation of their poverty unless the rich can at the same time be emancipated from the diseases – physical, moral and spiritual – of their wealth.'[18]

Liberalism through capitalism promotes ambition. At the root of liberalism is economic success. 'If you work hard enough and develop your skills you will succeed. Of course others will not. But your primary concern is your own wellbeing.'

Liberal thinking calls people 'to be more by having more' while Christ calls people 'to be more by loving more'. It is clear that liberalism becomes the greatest contradiction to Christianity. 'When we develop a social situation which foments the idea that being more is having more, we are producing a cirrhosis of the heart. In time the heart becomes so hardened that the word of God will not be able to permeate it.'[19]

Such thinking is a challenge to our traditional understanding of the gospel. The individualism of our faith has contributed to the competitive, success orientation of both ourselves and our society. All education is geared to mesh with the spirit of competitive self-achievement. At the heart of Christian theology is grace – free, unmerited, self-giving. It is a gift of God. The heart of Christian ethics is gratitude – the expression of gratitude given in love and joyful service. Grace and gratitude are currently in short supply. Love and gratitude are not expressed most effectively in competition, nor individually. Both demand to be shared. The gospel of Christ speaks about better things; the healing of relationships; the cessation of violence; of people living in harmony. Whenever human relationships are devalued a fundamental human need is ignored – the need to love and to be loved. The words of the commandment include both 'self love' and 'love of neighbour'. They are not to be dismissed, both are integral to understanding God's

purpose for humanity, revealing the roots of spiritual understanding that exist in all people.

Choosing to resist the bomb

Our religious thinking in the First World is substantially
untouched by the pain of the Third World. In our worship we
rarely allow their needs to be uppermost. When we do reflect
on the hungry, to what extent do we also reflect on the failure
of our Western affluence to face the problem of hunger?
'Instead of feeding the hungry, we in the First World arm
ourselves against them. . . "the bombs are falling now," states
the US Peace Group Mobilization for Survival.'[20]

Militarism is integral to the capitalist structure. What we have
must be protected, whatever the cost. Militarism dominates our
national and international thinking. It creates the need for
enemies and is exposed in the arms trade, nuclear over-kill
capacity and deterrents of all kinds. The legacy of individualism
has left the Church worldwide consistently refusing to condemn
militarism. The Church goes on tacitly condoning governments
who increase the potential for human annihilation every minute
of every day. The question such a refusal raises is, 'How can
we give our lives totally to God's life in the world if we do not
allow our vision of the nature and justice of God to interfere
with the powers that be?'

The bomb has become a catalyst for the Church. The present
social reality of nuclear weapons reveals the extent of the Christian capacity to trust God. There are Christians who see the
bomb as the ultimate weapon against communism. It is argued
that such weapons are a necessary protection, that they free
the gospel to wage war against communism. For others the
bomb has revealed all too starkly the extent to which faith in
God, limited by individualism, cannot reflect trust in God. Jim
Wallis has put it like this: 'A Church that places its trust in the
bomb is a Church that no longer trusts in the Lord'.[21] His
perception exposes the Church's vulnerability to compromise

and its failure to stand against what St. Paul has called 'the principalities and powers . . . the world rulers of this present darkness. . . the spiritual host of wickedness in the heavenly places' (Ephesians 6:13). Such powers are tangibly expressed in nuclear weapons, repression, hunger and the manipulation of currency and commodity prices which keep few rich and many poor.

The bomb is a catalyst for the Church because it reveals what little place renunciation and sacrifice have among us. The reliance of western Christians on political alliances and weapons systems for their protection, is reminiscent of the reliance that Zedekiah put on the armies of Egypt (Jeremiah 37), despite the prophet's pleas to return and trust the Lord. The prophetic dimension of Scripture shows us the struggle the Lord's people had throughout history in learning to trust God. Such struggles are integral to our own faith. The prophetic message is always one of renunciation, the giving up of pretence and misplaced security. Such renunciation is perceived as folly to everyone else. The supreme folly is the cross.

Choosing the resistance of the cross

The cross is both vulnerability and victory. In the first instance it is vulnerability. Jesus reveals the full implications of the Incarnation, and shows us that it is more than the sharing of our humanity, our life, our human lot. It meant becoming victim to the powerful, and suffering the dehumanising process of torture and death. 'Many people were shocked when they saw him, he was so disfigured that he hardly looked human' (Isaiah 52:13 GNB).

Within such vulnerability the true nature of the servant is revealed. The one who would serve the poor, captive, blind and oppressed, has faced the cost of their liberation. Standing before Pilate, Jesus reveals himself as subject to a Higher Power than Rome. Nevertheless, Jesus knew that the choices he had made would make him subject to the brutality of the cross (John 19:10–11).

The vulnerability of the cross reveals the judgement of the cross. To the poor, it is hope; Jesus is paying the cost of salvation, their salvation. Jesus stands beside them, himself victim, and provides together with solidarity, hope and forgiveness. To the rich and powerful who are in control, the cross reveals the true cost of salvation for them. In order that rich and poor should understand the value of human liberation to God, Jesus chose the path that would lead inexorably to the cross. The poor in all times have been unloved, devalued and dehumanised. The cross of Christ reveals God's unlimited love for them. The rich and powerful are trapped in their need to control resources, events and circumstances. The cross of Christ offers an alternative: the relinquishment of wealth and control in order to choose servanthood and humility.

The victory of the cross is expressed in ultimate terms by Isaiah: 'Many nations will marvel at him and kings will be speechless with amazement. They will see and understand something that they have never known' (Isaiah 52:14 GNB). The amazement is at the sheer power and simplicity of it all. Total, self-giving love becomes the weapon which 'disarms the principalities and powers. . . and makes a public example of them. . .' (Colossians 2:15). The illusions, lies and threats of the powerful are all exposed and vanquished by the power of the truth and love of God.

The resurrection expresses the victory of the cross in terms of the here and now. The cross spelt defeat, loss and failure. The resurrection reveals the cross to be the way in which the Kingdom will be established. It reveals the pattern of life for rich and poor, for all who would follow Jesus. The cross 'not only frees us from personal sin; it also liberates us from the powers of this world. Living freely in relationship to those powers and establishing a moral independence from them will ultimately lead to a cross'.[22]

Call to resistance

Resistance is at the heart of the cross and therefore of the Christian faith. As such it needs re-establishing at the centre of the Christian Church. This chapter invites people to choose resistance. It is not a call for a new era of Christian political order. Neither is it a call for anarchy or anti-institutionalism. It is a call to choose to resist all that prevents the Kingdom of God emerging in this world. 'Though this world is not yet the Kingdom itself, it is the battleground and construction site of the Kingdom, which comes on earth from God himself. We could all relive now in the spirit of his Kingdom through new obedience and creative discipleship.'[23] The call to resist is a call for personal faith within the community of God's people. It is a call for the rejection of privatisation and individualisation of faith. It is a call for discipleship marked by quiet, strong determination that is without rancour or bitterness. This resistance will be expressed in joy and in hope. It will believe in the God who intervenes, but also in the cross of Christ and the power of his resurrrection. It will seek to conform to the way of Christ, expressing itself in solidarity with all that seeks to exploit and annihilate. It will accept the consequences of its actions whether they are accepted or rejected by the institutions. It will not seek power for itself and will be marked by a life lived in community and fraternal love.

Notes

1. *The other side of 1984*, Lesslie Newbiggin: BCC, p. 34.
2. *Ibid.*, p. 35.
3. *On Human Dignity*, Jurgen Moltmann: SCM, p. 66. Moltmann's essay on Luther's doctrine of the two Kingdoms is worth taking time to study in detail. I have only summarised it.
4. *Ibid.*, p. 68.
5. *Ibid.*, p. 71.
6. *Ibid.*, p. 75.
7. *Ibid.*, p. 75.
8. *Constructing Local Theologies*, Robert Schreiter: SCM, p. 5.
9. 'Standing at the end of the eurocentric area of Christianity', J B Metz: *Doing Theology in a Divided World*, Orbis, p. 88.
10. 'Methodology for West European Theology of Liberation', *Doing Theology in a Divided World*, *op. cit.* I am grateful for the individual statement of George Casalis that gave me this idea. I have used some of his phrases without quotative punctuation.
11. Casalis, *ibid.*, p. 107.
12. *The Emergent Church*, J B Metz: SCM, pp. 17, 18.
13. *Ibid.*, p. 18.
14. *Ibid.*, p. 18.
15. *Ibid.*, p. 24.
16. *Ibid.*, p. 27.
17. *Doing Theology in a Divided World*, *op. cit.*, p. 88.
18. *International Bulletin of Mission Research*, John Stam (vol. 9, no. 1. January 1985), p. 5.
19. *Ibid.*, p. 5.
20. Miguel d'Escoto – The various quotations that follow are from an interview which was syndicated to a number of magazines and newspapers. Quotations recorded here were in *Sojourners*.

21. *Landscape of Poverty*, *op. cit.*, p. 5.
22. *Doing Theology in a Divided World*, *op. cit.*, p. 82.
23. Moltmann, *op. cit.*, p. 109.

Chapter Ten

A God Who Speaks To The Church

God's people need an environment in which they can make choices to resist all that seeks to exploit, annihilate and prevent the revealing of the Kingdom of God. Such an environment is created when the *Bible*, *community, reality* together with *worship* are present. This environment will reveal God as one who acts within the day to day circumstances of human affairs. To see God in action demands the presence of three elements: first, the reality of God; secondly history and tradition, and thirdly what might be termed the present social reality – things as they are.

God reveals that he is real, because he speaks. Because God is reality, he speaks to reality. Nothing escapes God's word. No famine, no conflict or ideology, no ecology, no situation, person or nation is outside his word. In and as Jesus the word is revealed (John 1:14). Through Jesus God's purpose to 'reconcile all things to himself – things in heaven, and in earth and under the earth' (Colossians 1:20 RSV) is made effective. In speaking God puts the Bible, the teachings of the Church, events and circumstances, prophets and others who interpret the signs of the times at his disposal. God speaks into the experience of everyone.

Hearing God calls for listening and interpretation. To hear God he must first be listened to. Ways of hearing him include the Bible, prayer, tradition, events and circumstances. When God is heard to speak, he speaks to reality because he is concerned to transform it. When we hear God speak in the Scriptures for instance we may 'not find it congenial, consistent or significant. By all means raise these questions, but first, listen to the Word'.[1]

To illustrate how God acts I want to reflect on an experience that began in our lives thirteen years ago. It is a model, and because it is made up of ordinary sinful people, it is a far from perfect one.

A personal illustration

When I was first ordained I was involved in the planting of a new Church on a housing estate near Portsmouth. The way it was established was really quite conventional, although at the time it seemed innovative, exciting and new. However, there were distinguishing features that made it a unique situation. For many years a plot of land had been reserved for the building of a Church. It was the gift of the landowner, a local farmer, who had sold the rest of his land for a Council development. Part of the estate, the home-owner sector, had been completed years earlier. The sign in the field – 'site of new Church' – had long disappeared by the time we arrived. One resident told the Vicar, 'This estate has no soul – it is up to the Church to give it one.'

There were no other Churches within the locality of the estate. The Parish Church, under whose auspices the initiative to plant a Church was made, met the rites of passage needs, but was geographically difficult for casual attendance. Our work began after some initial canvassing by volunteer visitors from the Parish Church. I visited several hundred homes over the next few months. In an attempt to consolidate relationships Dee, to whom I am married, and I opened our home for informal evenings. We invited all the people that we had met in a given street or block. The response surprised us both, and

I think the many who came. People who had lived, often for years, in the same street, were meeting each other as neighbours for the first time.

From these contacts and the painstaking building of relationships a decision was made to invite people to a weekly service to be held in a local school. Once again the response was both surprising and overwhelming. Few had any knowledge of the Bible, the sayings of Jesus or of liturgy. Most had little intimate contact with the Church in any way at any time. What became clear early on was that God was speaking to the reality in which these people lived. He spoke to the isolation, the need for neighbourliness, the longing for community, for something more in life than a house, a car and two kids. God speaks to reality because God is reality. He speaks to the experience of everyone. He seeks people where they are.

We began our learning of the gospel by reading and talking it through as it had been interpreted by St Mark. Everyone was given a gospel and encouraged to bring it each time they came. One grandfather sat down on the afternoon of his first visit and read it cover to cover. He then proceeded to read it to his daughter and granddaughter. Traditionally the scriptures have been understood as one way in which God speaks. As we read St. Mark we tried to earth what we were reading in our own situation, the circumstances and events that were happening around us and were part of our lives. The sermon – if it could be called such – was both reading, teaching and discussion. We found it calling us to a commitment to Jesus' way of doing and being. Simply yet profoundly we discovered the reality of God is revealed in the Word – Jesus. As we understood that experience more and more we committed ourselves to God in Christ and found a commitment to one another and the circumstances of our neighbourhood. Among the events and circumstances of our neighbourhood were: a new estate growing threateningly on the other side of the lane; the mystery of suffering, expressed in cancer and mental illness; a sense of isolation and loneliness; stress both in work and family.

Pastoral care and welcome of the stranger became natural expressions of a faith that was seeking to understand God and his love as revealed through the living word, the written word and the events and circumstances of our lives. Fear over the new estate and the 'kind of people' it would bring was tantamount to paranoia. One neighbour of ours bought Alsatians to defend herself from the marauders who she was convinced would arrive in the first furniture wagon. In reality the first to arrive were a poor young couple whose baby was shortly to die a cot death.

We discovered that God speaks through prophets and others who interpret the signs of the times. Part of our prophetic role – though undoubtedly we did not understand it as such – was to cross the barriers of prejudice and fear with hope and acceptance. By making the stranger welcome in an alien environment, allowing them to feel safe and at home, people filled that role. As the curtains appeared in windows so representatives of the Church appeared at the door. On occasion the welcome was enriched with flowers, gifts of cake or tea. People were touched by the simplicity and love of it all. God was speaking to the experience of everyone – whether they knew it or not. We were discovering in very simple ways the profound truth that God reveals himself as one who reconciles.

For a time the experience had echoes of the post-Pentecost experience described in Acts 2. People were eating in each other's houses, discussing, praying, reading the scriptures, breaking bread and sharing meals together. They held public services in the shopping precinct and made friends with the people who were moving into their new homes. For a time a Church 'enjoyed the goodwill of all the people' (Acts 2:47). What was significant about our experience then was that we learned that when God speaks, he also has to be listened to.

Throughout that time, groups gathered in homes to learn more and discover worship together. We learned early on that we had to listen to each other, to share our story and history. It was a time for sharing dreams, hopes, fears, our sense of failure and disillusionment. We learned to laugh and to cry, to wrestle with guilt and experience forgiveness. We recognised our confusion over suffering and death. We felt the limitations of our tradition of class and culture. We learned to celebrate our differences. At times we were together, at others apart. We experienced powerlessness. Whatever our personal history and tradition the context in which we now lived was changing our understanding of the reality of God.

One occasion that made us feel powerless and angry was when a young mother died of cancer. We coped with that by being angry with God as well as praying to him. Then in response to the compassion that was stirred in us, we turned to caring for her husband and family. One woman was moved to offer herself as a Care Assistant to the terminally ill. The history and the tradition of the estate said 'there is nothing we can do' – the reality of God among us, despite our anger and confusion, said 'there is a better way'.

A further occasion of powerlessness happened when the Council decided to re-route the main road through the estate into a quiet, narrow, residential street. Yellow lines were painted, trees lopped – all without consultation. We recognised – intuitively I hasten to add – that what the Council was doing was a result of its history and tradition. If Councils – one of the lower principalities and powers – have been allowed to act without consultation or objection, then such history quickly passes into tradition. It is worth noting here that all the circumstances of our lives are routed in history and tradition. Capitalism and communism, those two competing models of human control, have come about through a historical process and contribute to our present reality.

It is easy to believe that the effects of history and tradition, whether personal or social, are unchangeable. Such a view is one 'of history's so called "invisible forces". Many people feel that things have been more or less the way they are today; that our world has been organised and structured this way since the beginning of time. Such an understanding could easily lead to total acceptance of the status quo as our world would be seen to be unchangeable. An analysis of history, however, shows that much of the present reality has been man-made and not been given by God. Consequently it leads to a very different understanding of what is and what is not changeable. This in turn leads to a whole different action towards changing the present reality'.[2]

We hadn't worked all this out when we protested to the Council and fought for change, and then for a subequent change to the alternative they foisted upon us! What we were learning, as much in the community as the Church, is that in all social reality 'there is a tension between the tendency to isolation and the tendency to become involved'.[3] For Christians that tension is resolved when they have discovered how they see God in relation to the world. If we see ourselves as having no responsibility because 'here we have no abiding city' then we may tend to isolate ourselves from the changing of things. If on the other hand 'we see our task as building the Kingdom of God, of moving this world a little closer to where God wishes it to be then we will logically become involved in the process of building the Kingdom and commitment to this involvement will grow'.[4]

Before concluding this recollection, I want to say that what happened among us happened to us all together. One of our local teachers said, 'It doesn't feel like Church as we have known it in the past . . . we feel that you, like us, are learning and puzzling it out as we go along.' How true! Somehow too, those who had begun to worship together on Sundays and share their lives together during the week included in their thinking and acting the rest of the community.

All was not roses! Many people had too much thrust upon them too soon, some took too much upon themselves. Others came and found it all too much. Others found it too little, in the sense that much of what was happening amongst us, was happening at a time when the charismatic renewal was being experienced in more established Churches. Some from neighbouring parishes decided to come and worship with us because they sensed the Spirit stirring among us. Initially many were disappointed because they were expecting the charismatic patterns being experienced elsewhere. We suffered the charge of being 'too woolly' or worse still, unsound! What was happening was indeed 'charismatic' but it was among a people who had no tradition to throw off and no expectation of what 'might' or 'should' be.

Of course, it would be good to say that the theological development of this Church began without any cultural clutter. It was not so, and really, it never could be. From the beginning, our understanding of the gospel was deeply coloured by the culture in which we grew and lived. Being an estate on the outskirts of a naval port, many worked in both the Marines, Navy and associated technological and service industries. Attitudes to peace and war, unions and management, law and order, race and class and, to some extent, women were predictable enough. Any attempt to see the gospel related to the wider issues of the bomb, racism and social justice would produce 'pinko-commie-language' at once! Yet strangely enough the practical reality of caring for the Vietnamese boat people and supporting people in the community out of work came as part of the rhythm of life. At that time I was myself not particularly committed to seeing peace and justice as fundamental to the gospel we preach. It was part of my pilgrimage that was yet to be.[5] Like most people facing conflict, or potential conflict, the tendency was to run from it rather than to hold it in tension, allowing for the process of conversion which had begun in other areas of our lives to take its course.

It was at this point in our experience that two things occurred: one, a growing conviction that only some form of small structured community network could take us significantly forward; and two, an invitation for me to join the community at Scargill as Chaplain. We chose the latter to help ourselves understand more about community.

Bible study groups have a time-honoured place, particularly

in evangelical and charismatic tradition, though increasingly in all theological groupings in the Church, and, since Vatican II, with considerable impact in the Roman Catholic Church. It is the nearest experience that many Christians have to community.

The Bible from above

Within our tradition of Bible study there has been a tendency to focus in two places. First, people come together to read the Bible and pray. Their primary purpose in meeting is to study and reflect on the scriptures, and then to seek to make use of the knowledge gained in their personal lives as Christians. Secondly, other groups come together to meet and study the Bible for itself. They look for meaning in events such as the stories of Abraham, Joseph or Moses. Some look for answers to philosophical and historical questions. Questions about the meaning and nature of God. The second type of group rarely seeks to make links with the experience of its members or the events that surround their lives. This kind of study is usually subject to the limitations of time and duration, and becomes 'a Bible study course'. It has a limited objective and a limited life. It is essentially the Bible 'read from above'.

Our approach to Bible study is a source of bewilderment to those who belong to base communities. Peter Batangan (see page 67) said he could see in Britain no attempt to perceive the Bible as 'our story', 'our history'. Our failure to make connections between people and events in the scriptures and relationships and events in the present, surprised him. He observed we set no tasks or projects within our Bible study groups. We made no attempt to see whether what we read and understood had any bearing in terms of action on real life situations. He expressed the view that no attempt would be made in a Base Community to move on to another passage of scripture without first fulfilling the task laid upon the group by the previous passage.

The Bible from below

At the Selly Oak consultation in 1983, Dean Ian Fraser gave an example of the way the Bible came to life in a Basic Community in the Philippines. A small coastal village had traditional rights to the local sea fishing. The village landlord owned a fish farm which the villagers depended upon for their livelihood when the sea fishing was poor. One day the landlord went and hired cheap labour to manage his fish farm. At about the same time, Japanese fishermen with large trawlers began fishing the traditional fishing grounds. As the villagers studied the New Testament in their groups – the fishermen who toiled all night and caught nothing (Luke 5:5); the parables of landlords and unjust stewards; the unjust Judge (Luke 18:1–8) – their identification was real. 'This is us, this is our story,' they said. From the point of identification sprang the possibility of change. First the promise of hope. The fishermen's recognition of the Lord is important to their hope of a livelihood in both past, present and future. Secondly the recognition that landlords have always been capable of manipulating things to their advantage needed to be acknowledged. Thirdly that justice could be achieved through prayer and action (Luke 18:1–8) needed to be recognised as the villagers struggled on in faith and hope.

We might call such a way of reading the Bible, 'reading from below'. Much of the Bible study which we do demands considerable general knowledge before it can be engaged in with any degree of understanding. In part this is because no one likes to appear ignorant. It also has to do with the way we have traditionally learned things. Teacher-pupil models last for most of our adult lives. The Bible study leader who has read his commentaries and prepared his notes and questions is ready, when he meets the group, to play 'guess what I'm thinking'. This approach to Bible study is much like the one-sided sermon. How much we need to experiment with reading the Bible together, even in Church services, having a short exposition, and then reflecting on its relevance by discussion and interchange, then choosing to act on it.

Recently our Church has begun an experiment in reading the gospel of Luke from below. The group is comprised of many who have recently been baptised and confirmed as adults and others who are interested in trying such an approach. Partly because of the range of experience and understanding in the group, we have agreed on some ground rules. In the first instance we have agreed to try not to anticipate how the story will unfold. We have begun with the story of Zacharias and Elizabeth. Secondly we have agreed that if anyone can throw light on the 'story so far' with appropriate examples from the Old Testament, they are permitted to do so. Thirdly, we have agreed to try to understand the meaning of phrases like 'God my saviour . . .' (Luke 1:47) or 'peace to men who enjoy his favour' (Luke 2:14) – as they would have been understood at the time. Fourthly, we have agreed to allow the story so far to touch base with the experience of our own lives and encounters. Fifthly we have agreed to struggle together to perform a task that the gospel sets before us – week in week out. It is too early in the day to know how it will develop, but already it has enabled everyone to take part and identify.

Carlos Mesters in his seminar on the Bible, given at the International Ecumenical Congress in Sao Paolo in 1980, interprets the experience of believers in Base Communities as revealing three elements in their interpretation of the Bible. 'The Bible itself, the community, and reality (ie. the real life situation of the people and the surrounding world). With these three elements they seek to hear what the word of God is saying. And for them the word of God is not just the Bible. The word of God is within reality and it can be discovered there with the help of the Bible. When one of these three elements is missing, however, interpretation of the Bible makes no progress and enters into crisis. The Bible loses its function.'[6]

The Base Communities have something to teach us about reading the Bible and interpreting it in our own situation. The starting points at which we allow God's word to speak into the real life situation are various. It doesn't matter where people begin hearing God speak, in the context of the family or community, within everyday problems and hopes or in the Bible itself. What is essential is that all three elements are required in order to hear God speak.

It is quite a struggle to hear God's word speak with authority and be reflected in the nature and quality of the lives we live. We often come to the Bible with such profound preconceptions that God's word is limited in what it can say to us.

The Bible in text and context

There is a growing need for us to grasp what a given text, sentence, symbol or story meant when it was first recognised as the word of God. For how and why a text was given initially will effect how we interpret it today. We need to see texts in their original historical context. Then we can allow these texts to speak to us in the present for the future. 'For the word does not come to us as texts, but through texts as a living person'.[7]

As we come to the Bible, two things become clear. First, the promise of God in history, and second the history of human hope. God's promise is liberation. He liberates people 'from their inner and outer prisons – Israel from Egypt, Jesus from death and the Church from the nations'.[8] God's promise is always expressed in action, and such action has provided the ground for hope in human history. As people reflect on God's promise fulfilled so the history of human hope develops.

Much of what is now the Bible is the result of the memory of the people. For people of the Bible, memory is essential. We are not talking here about 'memorising texts'. We are talking about the corporate memory of a people who have told and retold their story and history. Such memory keeps hope alive. The recalling of the past into the present. It was as the people of Israel recalled events that marked liberation for them, Passover, crossing the Red Sea, being sustained forty years in the desert and so forth, that they could keep hope alive when all was dark. No study of the Bible is complete without recalling to mind the promise of God in history, for that is what enables us to go on hoping in history.

As we grasp this principle of hope, by recalling this past, and allowing that memory to shape our hope, so we shall see how risky it is dealing with a God of promise in the history of human hope. The Magnificat declares the political implications of a God of promise – the mighty removed from their thrones, the poor, the humble and meek lifted up. Hungry people get fed, rich people get sent away empty-handed. The powerful are threatened and the powerless are given hope. The God of the past is concerned with human liberation, with justice, with harmony in a real world of flesh and blood. Can he be any less concerned for the present and the future?

The Bible as a truth-revealing environment

I have been deeply challenged as I have engaged with the Communities in Ireland and, by proxy, with the Base Communities in their growing understanding of the use of the Bible. Like many I have found it easy to say 'everybody has a different view on what the Bible teaches – for instance Jesus and politics'. It is so much easier to defend what we think we know to be the truth rather than expose ourselves to a dialogue that brings us to truth. We must learn to question the seemingly obvious with openness and honesty. So much of what we see as obvious comes about because of the theological, cultural and ideological pre-suppositions we bring to what we read in scripture. We need to develop a keen sense for opinions that masquerade as biblical, but are in reality socio-political.

Nicaraguan evangelicals have provided a valuable illustration about dialogue that brings us to truth. When the Samoza régime was first overthrown, evangelicals were taught to be suspicious of the new Sandinista government. Some members were disciplined by the Church if they had participated in the overthrow of Samoza. Soon evangelicals discovered that the Sandinistas were achieving in literacy, housing, education and health services what they as Christians were not even talking about. They also had to face the fact that discussions were taking place with the revolutionary government that were not on the agenda of most Christians – justice, institutional violence, and the violence that sprang from counter-revolution. Issues such as the mission of the Church, faith and ideology were all on the agenda of the government. Such was the impact of the revolution that it provoked the comment from a Chilean theologian, Pablo Richard – 'Never in the history of revolution had the Church enjoyed such opportunities as it now possessed in the Nicaraguan revolutionary process.'[9] Evangelicals moved to a place of repentance and co-operation with the government.

One of the most moving testimonies of the word of God being heard and practised, followed the immediate success of the Sandinistas. Commandante Tomas Borge ordered the release from post-war detention of the National Guard who had supported Samoza. It was a costly decision for many went to support those who have now become the Contras, seeking to overthrow the government. Tomas visited the jail where former Samozan torturers were interned. Among these was a man who had personally and brutally tortured Tomas himself, a man notorious for his cruelty. On arrival at the prison, Tomas said to him, 'Remember when I told you I would take revenge when I was free? I now come for my revenge. For your hate and torture I give you love, and for what you did I give you freedom.' The man went free. 'Forgiving,' as Borge said elsewhere, 'is for us a revolutionary virtue.'

To hear God's word the Church cannot stand still. We must allow scripture to go on correcting its misunderstandings of God, of ourselves, of our cultural inheritance, our ideology and above all, of how God speaks. We must allow the Bible to speak to new circumstances and to challenge us afresh. Christians must let God be God – 'confessing that if God exists at all, God lives independently, though not in isolation from their intelligence, longing, insight, or their interpretations, even those which divine the truth. They must be open to God's initiative.'[10]

The environment of reality

During 1984 I attended a course at St. George's House, Windsor. One of the keynote speakers was Ronald Higgins, author of *The Seventh Enemy*. In essence he argued that there were seven main threats to humanity's survival – population explosion, food shortage, scarcity of natural resources, pollution and degradation of the environment, nuclear energy, uncontrolled technology, moral blindness and political inertia. He says: 'We and our children are approaching a world of mounting confusion and horror. The next twenty-five years, possibly the next decade, will bring starvation to hundreds of millions, and hardship, disorder and war to most of the rest of us. Democracy, where it exists, has little chance of survival, nor in the longer run has our industrial way of life. There will not be a "better tomorrow" beyond our present troubles. That may sound hysterical. Yet it is what the evidence would seem to suggest.' In essence, what Higgins argued was that because of 'moral blindness and political inertia', there is not sufficient will to create alternatives to deal with the other six threats. Hence the seventh enemy.

Whether Higgins is an undue pessimist or not remains to be seen. He is certainly not alone in his thinking. No one seriously denies that the North is in crisis as much as the South; the East as the West. I am not a sociologist or social analyst, but the present social reality for all but a dwindling few is crisis.[11] To this the Church must give its *will*, its mind and all its resources, or else it must be subsumed along with everything else.

The phrase 'the global village' enjoyed a certain popularity a decade or so ago. In essence it sought to express the reality of our planet, that all are much nearer than we thought and each needs the other in order to survive. In Christian terms this is true. The Third World Church, often in poverty and oppression, is experiencing a phenomenal growth and influence. It is increasingly clear that we cannot shape our own future without reference to what they are experiencing and understanding. Equally we cannot ignore them economically and socially. If we allow our sisters and brothers to go hungry because of our greed and our insistence on maintaining a life-style that by its nature is oppressive, do we not in fact break fellowship with them at the Eucharist?

Equally, if we do not learn to challenge existing structures, are we not simply agreeing with Higgins and accepting that as Christians too, we are victims of moral, spiritual and political blindness? Is not that very inertia a mark of our dependence as a people?

In endeavouring to understand how we learn from the Base Communities, J B Metz has argued that what is needed is the 'transformation of a dependent people'.[12] Choosing to exercise will and live with the consequences is the first step in adult behaviour. By channelling our will into the 'will to resist' we set in motion the transformation process. Transformation begins when we take the God and Father of the crucified, risen, ascended Christ seriously, through the power of the Holy Spirit. But we have to choose it and to will it. 'It is here at home first that we must face up to imperialism, militarism, capitalism, oppression in all its forms . . .' (and our material affluence). It is here *at home* that we must identify and face into exploitation in terms of unemployment, racism, violence both institutional and criminal. 'It is here *at home* we must struggle against the arms race, that murderous folly that each year, without open war, occasions the death of millions by starvation . . . that emasculates and savages the economies of the First, Second and Third Worlds together and causes us who are rich to lose the meaning of life, and suffer instead a permanent, all-pervading anxiety.'[13]

Notes

1. 'Everything but the Bible', William Stringfellow: *Sojourners*, January 1986.
2. *Social Analysis in the Light of the Gospel*, Healy Reynolds: Fodens, pp. 6, 7.
3. *Op. cit.*, p. 7.
4. *Op. cit.*, p. 7.
5. See my contribution to 'Time to Choose' Celebration, *Personal Pilgrimage*, p. 91.
6. 'The Use of the Bible – Basic Christian Communities', Carlos Mesters: *Challenge of Basic Christian Communities 1*, Orbis.
7. *On Human Dignity*, Jurgen Moltmann: SCM, pp. 97–111.
8. *Ibid*.
9. *International Bulletin of Mission Research*, John Stam, (vol. 9, no. 1. January 1985), p. 5.
10. *Ibid*.
11. *The Seventh Enemy*, Ronald Higgins: Hodder & Stoughton.
12. The Emergent Church, J B Metz: SCM.
13. *Doing Theology in a Divided World*, *op. cit.*, p. 109.

Chapter Eleven

A New Way of Being The Church

A Paradigm Shift

The move from dependence in childhood to independence or interdependence, is the result of an exercise of the will. In Church and community terms, 'a dependent people has to transform itself, and not just behave like a people being taken care of. This is how "Basic Communities" emerge in the Church'.[1] What is required is something of a paradigm shift. James Robertson in *The Sane Alternative* tells us 'a paradigm shift is the change that takes place from time to time in a basic belief or assumption . . . underlying our perception and action'.[2] If, for instance, our basic belief about the Church is that it is an 'organised religious activity with a code of religious doctrines' – then it is a paradigm shift for it to become a 'community based on personal experience'.

For centuries the Church has mirrored the world's way of doing things. To minister in the Church, for example, has meant the acquisition of appropriate qualifications; the appointment to a position; the possession of a corpus of knowledge and spirituality that can be revered, thereby giving status. Above all such status and qualifications give one advantages over those less successful or able. With the shift to Church as 'community based on personal experience', such an emphasis is lessened.

Once again this is not necessarily an anti-academic or anti-clerical argument, it simply places such things in relation to the circumstances in which we find ourselves. Of course it raises the whole role of the professionally trained Minister or theologian – but maybe it also provides the clue to liberating him or her to the calling that they heard all along.

Bishops and others have a role in helping to effect this paradigm shift, but we must recognise that 'the transition from a paternalistic Church "taking care of people" to a maturer Church "of the people" does not simply come from above; in fact it cannot come from above at all.'[3] What needs stirring up is a revolution from below.

None of this is about founding a 'new Church'. It is not about forming 'House Churches' or 'Home Fellowships'. House Churches, at least in the United Kingdom, are schismatic by their very nature, separating themselves off from mainstream religion at points where they find it to be unacceptable or too worldly. Home Fellowships are simply too cosy a concept and they do not formulate sufficient commitment or the preaching of the word or have the Eucharist at the heart of their worship. David Clark in his seminal work *The Liberation of the Church*[4] has documented many other groups of people who form communities, some practising alternative lifestyles; others who are struggling to address everyday political life with a particular agenda, and of course the communities that seek to escape from reality.

The strength of Grassroots Communities is their continuing identification with and integration into the established Church order. This of course is not without its problems. Being Roman Catholic for the most part, the Eucharist is not celebrated unless a Priest is present. While not being 'a new Church' but rather 'a new way of being the Church', base communities nevertheless criticise the established Church when it fails to work for an environment of hope and freedom. In the first instance, therefore, the institutional Church needs to be made aware of the space in its arena of work which Base Communities could fill.

Working from what is

Part of the process by which a shift of emphasis comes about is the recognition of what is already happening. The model of a paternalistic Church does not fit into modern society. The growth of urban conurbations has never facilitated a Church with essentially rural parish structures. Many of the suburbs of our big cities, like Topsy, have simply 'just growed'. They and inner city areas were once parishes in little hamlets or villages. Where the Church once cared for the wellbeing of all, in educational as well as spiritual terms, that task is now substantially in the hands of the state. Services to mark rites of passage, within a growing multicultural and non-religious society, are on the decline. Most feel the Church to be unapproachable, and even when approachable incomprehensible.

In illustrating this last point I want again to refer to our Church planting experience. Despite the friendly welcome given to newcomers, few initially came to the Church. 'The Church' was in the school and had been established little more than a year. One afternoon I was visiting a young woman who said, 'You probably think we are awful not coming to Church. We have never felt so welcomed anywhere in our lives. But you see most of us feel we don't know anything about God and that, and besides we wouldn't want to look silly not knowing what to do.' Our response to this, was to form a group which would start from where they were.[5]

There is little in our religion that brings genuine consolation. Part of the reason for this lies in the expectation that 'Father will look after us, comfort us, and console us'. 'You are here,' said a parishioner, 'to look after us and care for us all.' Genuine consolation and caring is of value only when it is mutual, something in which all share. Who cares for the carers in our present structures? Do they care for themselves? If the incidents of marriage break-ups, loss of faith and nervous breakdowns among the clergy are anything to go by – no-one cares.

In practical terms one step forward would be a recognition by all participants in Church life of their mutual responsibility towards each other. Many parishes and Churches, including our own, have tried this as an organisational exercise with varying degrees of success. The chief contribution to either success or failure lies in the acceptance or rejection of personal responsibility towards each other. Again it is a question of the individual and the collective will.

Opportunities such as we had of planting a Church do not happen often. Most have to deal with things as they are. 'The Church cannot dissolve and choose for itself new members; the bearers and motive forces for the coming Church do not fall from heaven; they are in the first place (although not exclusively) members of the Church and professing Christians of today.'[6]

Nevertheless it is individuals collectively that will have to give the motivation and desire for change. The importance of personal experience and the confidence to assert it together are the means by which change is initiated. Also needed is a conversion to the belief that things could change, or even should change. That change will incorporate the conversion of our economic, social and political attitudes, as well as a re-examination of our faith. Jim Wallis calls us to see 'living, breathing, loving communities of faith at the local Church level as the foundation for all our answers'. It is within these that conversion takes place, for in them 'the translation of persons from one world to another takes place. It is inviting people into an environment where it becomes possible to live the Christian life'.[7]

A new meeting place of gospel and politics

We saw in Luther's doctrine of the two Kingdoms the inadequacy of the position that separates religion and politics. There is a need for a fresh point of meeting, in a manner that has been enfleshed by the experience of Basic Communities. Of course the fear of bringing politics into religion exists almost universally in the Western Church. There is a preference for keeping things on a 'purely spiritual' level, with an apparent neutrality over political matters. We fear things that will disturb our peace. Yet 'the high price we are paying in our parish communities for this kind of social indifference and pretended political neutrality become even more clear'.[8] The violence, unemployment and social deprivation of our own national life should be reason enough for us to engage through work and prayer in political struggle. Not to mention the hungry of the world, and those who live in terror of our weaponry. No movement on its own could engage in all these areas. Many people have already engaged in aspects of these things: the Peace Movement in its variety of forms; ecology groups; women's groups, War on Want, Tearfund, Christian Aid, Oxfam and the like. A friend of mine recently commented, 'I sometimes wonder if we are going to have time to save this generation.' Should that remark not act to spur us on?

The Church as a sign of the Kingdom needs to re-engage with the vision of community which Jesus modelled, and the early Church followed. Witnessing groups down the centuries have seen it as the place of resistance. We need to offer hope in the face of a worsening social, economic, ecological and political situation. 'The Church as Basic Community would now have the opportunity, in the situation of transition, of functioning not as a late arrival on the scene, but rather as an advance herald of something new, and this would be essential if we are to resist in kind the threatening barbarism. . .'[9] Now that is exciting!

A prophetic vision

Basic Communities are providing a prophetic voice for the Western Church. It is a prophetic voice which is also relevant.

J B Metz has directed us to three prophetic services which the poor Churches can offer to our situation. First, they show us the place of solidarity among persons. In the simplicity of neighbourhoods Christian people witness, worship, pray and speak into their own situation. The problem of 'individualism' which confronts us does not confront them. We see response to God in primarily individual terms, and the Holy Spirit as a gift for use in our personal life and relationships. They tend to see 'turning to Christ as a constant and lifetime process which encompasses all our activities. . . and the work of the Holy Spirit is in the community as a whole and in the world'. We need this additional dimension, and perhaps the Communities need something of the dimensions we have. Andrew Kirk, Theologian Missioner of the Church Missionary Society (CMS), sees a breakthrough in these terms: 'Both in their different ways stress the need for serious commitment to Jesus Christ – Protestants emphasise He is Saviour, the Communities that He is Lord. If the genuinely biblical practices could be brought together the Churches . . . would be more faithful to their calling.'[10]

Learning solidarity demands unlearning our individualism. But solidarity is not the denial of the personal, it is the recognition of the need for the whole person to be incorporated. This is expressed in mutual help, deeper and more stable lives, joy in sharing common life and common tasks. With that sharing comes also that conscious participation in pursuing common values, towards a common commitment and mission. Solidarity does not deny the need for affirming individual identity. Co-responsibility and the sense of belonging to and with others, does not mean total absorption. That is totalitarianism – not community. It is when people are in relationship with each other that gifts of leadership are called forth. The gift of the poet, the prophet and the teacher. Within community, people can raise questions and struggle with answers. A group of people can come to a common mind on issues and matters that affect the mission of the Church. All too often questions remain undiscussed and their implications for the mission of the Church are not worked out.

'A second gift is a new connection between salvation and liberation, between the experience of grace and freedom, between mysticism and politics as opposed to our prevailing separation of these realities. . .'[11] We need to re-interpret words that have become familiar to us. So equally we need to feel the load that each word, such as salvation, or liberation, grace or freedom has to bear. We see salvation in essentially mystical terms, and liberation in essentially political terms. Yet both concepts exist in tension and mutual interdependence in the scriptures. Grace is a gift of freedom ergo freedom is a gift of grace. Both have their mystical and political place, neither one to the exclusion of the other. This is the single most important part of this second prophetic gift: that God is concerned with wholeness.

The third gift is that which brings a political dimension to our gospel and Church life. It is a hard gift to accept but we ought to ask – 'What have we really achieved with our "purely spiritual" parish communities?' After one of my early sermons on the 'bomb as catalyst for the Church', I was taken to task for introducing politics into the pulpit. The same person who took me to task subsequently canvassed me on behalf of a political party for the forthcoming general election! Political neutrality is not a reality within the Church. But the politics we are talking of are not those of a party, whether or not a particular party espouses a concern we share as God's people. Politics is to do with being governed. The Church's governor is God, the ruler of the Kingdom of God. We cannot duck the political implications of this and the question continues to raise its head, 'Who do we serve; who is God for us?'

Equally we must ask if our 'purely religious Church' has brought us a living experience of peace and joy and a fellowship overflowing with love and consolation? Isn't the reality that people have got lost in organisation and feel isolated from real warmth and caring? The decline of religious activity within the Churches leaves us with few options if we are to make a constructive contribution to the future. If we see Basic Communities as an expression of the Church only in 'under-developed countries', then we shall be missing the essential challenge of them. If we can raise our game sufficiently to see their prophetic message as that which inspires us to look to God and transform ourselves from being a dependent people, then we can be a sign to the Church and to the world that is communitarian, prophetic and liberating.

I am aware of the difficulties. Equally I am aware of the present reality. Once again what is being argued is not anarchic or anti-institutional. Let us look at how we might go ahead from here.

A new ministry

While the majority of the parish Churches in the UK have attendances below a hundred, many congregations of two or three hundred people continue to exist. These gather Sunday by Sunday. The numbers preclude the formation of meaningful community association. Many passengers are carried. 'Commit-ment', even in the places where such a word has a high currency, is in reality low, rarely exceeding more than fifty per cent of the congregation. In Churches of that size the gap between the leadership and the person in the pew is enormous. Most feel that they cannot compete with the expertise and professionalism of the leadership. Many feel they are gifted but there is no room for them to exercise their gifts, particularly on the scale that seems to be required. Many see House Groups or Fellowships as a way forward. I would not want to demean such efforts, but they lack the nature of the Church in sign-ificant aspects. Such groups meet in evenings during the mid-week, and as not all can attend, membership is thus restricted. Andrew Kirk has pointed out that House Groups 'lack the main attributes of being a Church – a community drawn toge-ther around the preaching of the word and the celebration of the sacraments'.[12] Numerically such groups are too fragile. Basic Communities are sized between twenty-five and forty in number, including women, men and children. They are specifically intended to function within the neighbourhood. They are not seen as eclectic groups.

Significant and fundamental to Basic Communities is local leadership. Such leadership needs to be strong, not in an aggressive sense but in a way that helps people to get together, share values and concerns, and see how things can be changed. It is leadership concerned with interaction rather than reaction. It is about accepting certain values and ways of doing things together.

The key to this leadership is that it is local. Such leadership is essential to the development of Basic Communities. Leaders themselves will be aware of their locality. They will understand how important it is to meet the needs of belonging and loving, of self-esteem and self-actualisation. Experiments of indigenous leadership in Anglican Churches in Urban Priority Areas have been limited, but have usually resulted in some kind of course leading to ordination. Further experimentation in this area is planned through what will be known as 'locally ordained ministry'. However, it is to misunderstand the nature of leadership in Basic Communities to see it simply as priestly or presidential in function.

Communities call for and call forth all kinds of gifts and ministries. It is not envisaged that everyone tries their hand at everything. That is romantic twaddle! Communities must reveal the prophet, the poet, the teacher, the pastor and the songwriter. They will reflect the mood and spirit of the community as expressed in its life, worship and action. Communities, though not lacking in structure, seek to develop minimal structures to promote maximum living. The talents, gifts and ministries of all members are the guarantee for this. One of the key gifts would be that of co-ordinator or convener of community.

Communities will reveal different ways of making decisions. Andrew Kirk says 'indigenous leadership can only be fostered. . . if local people know that they are responsible from first to last for the life and mission of the local Christian community'.[13] Living community is a process under God of learning, sharing, making decisions and taking risks. Basic Communities engage in social analysis. They learn to feel the pulse of the neighbourhood and ask questions. They learn to listen to the neighbourhood and through Bible study, worship and action, minister to it. The substance of their concern will be reflected as they break bread together. All kinds of models for social analysis are appearing, but a simple option might be based on the parish audit of *Faith in the City*.[14] We cannot hope to be 'leaven' if we do not know what we are supposed to be leavening.

Communities of this kind are outward looking. They provide a place of encounter with the unchurched and alienated. Their involvement in the neighbourhood, in local concerns and issues, in the organising and petitioning of Councils and governments makes them a front-line group for sharing Good News. They are the place where the casually baptised may be drawn into a deeper turning to Christ, entering with others in that process.

New roles for the clergy

The local Minister or parochial clergyman would gain a new role in Basic Community orientated Churches. Though of course not all will accept a model of community life. Communities are not to be seen as separate from the parish, they are part and pulse of it. In most traditions the celebration of the Eucharist is a priestly or presbyterial function. This would, initially at least, take on greater significance. Celebration of the Eucharist is central to both Church and Basic Community life. The Minister as President would have fresh significance.

Nevertheless, I believe this to be an interim – albeit a long interim – measure. While holding on to the view that the centre of Community life should always be the Eucharist, increase in the frequency of its celebration would cause significant problems. Episcopally ordained Ministers are in diminishing numbers and this already presents a practical problem for the Church in many areas. This problem would be increased with the development of Communities. Recognition of all ministries by episcopal Churches would help. So too, would the reserved sacrament or extended communion approach to the distribution of the Eucharist. However, this is of essence second best, and ignores the autonomous nature of communities within a wider structure. Metz argues, 'Properly speaking, the leader of such a Basic Community and the president at the celebration of the Lord's Supper should be able to come forth out of that community itself . . . certainly . . . such leaders . . . should not need to have religion alone as their profession in society; they would have to be able to exercise a secular profession alongside their Church ministry, something which is practically non-existent among us and scarcely seems to be desired.'[15] Of course such an issue raises more questions – but they should be discussed.

Communities need theology and they need theologians. The insight and power that has arisen from many communities' reflections upon experience and the scriptures, has prompted the Community itself to become the prime author of theology in local situations. 'The Holy Spirit works in and through the believing Community giving shape and expression to Christian experience.'[16] This serves to remind us that theology is not the property of a theological elite – it is like liturgy – faith seeking understanding among the people.

'Being a theologian is a gift requiring sensitivity to the context, an extraordinary capacity to listen, and an immersion in the scriptures and the experience of other Churches.'[17] The training of clergy is essentially theological, rather than pastoral or homiletical. Many are trained theologians, a process that is continuous and needs updating. Thus there is always a risk of separation from the Community. However it is folly for Communities to ignore the resources of a professional theologian, preferring ignorance to knowledge. As the prophet, poet or teacher seeks to interpret the experience of the Community, so the theologian has the task of helping the Community clarify its role, and relate it to the wider Church, both past and present. An essential part of the limited, but indispensable task of the theologian is to 'create bonds of mutual accountability between local and world Church'.[18] This I believe to be a significant function for local Ministers and Priests.

Church in nucleus

Basic Communities are 'the Church in nucleus'. They have a relationship that is significant both to other nuclei and to the parish, Diocese and wider Church. In episcopal tradition the Bishop is seen as the symbol of unity, and if, as in the Roman Catholic Diocese of Brentwood, the whole Diocese is being encouraged to develop a Basic Community, that symbolism holds good. But equally in the early Church Bishops were thicker on the ground than they are today. Properly understood the Parish Priest or local Minister, in a non-conformist tradition, could act as 'Bishop' to a community of Communities. Few would deny these days that both parish Minister and Bishops are sadly distanced from their people by the weight of administration. The Community structure would in time release something of that burden, because the conventional pastoral function would change.

Bishops, a sign of unity

The role of pastoral figures like Bishops or Presbyters is necessary for good order in the Church. In being the 'sign of unity', the Bishop will, with the help of others, co-ordinate and encourage; serve, teach, guide, govern – though not autocratically; approve actions and decisions of Communities affecting the wider Church; relate to the wider Church, and relate the wider Church to the Community. This task should be ecumenical. The development of Basic Communities, if it is to be in neighbourhoods, would be most effective ecumenically.

Within the United Kingdom the role of Bishops is unique. Many have traditional rights to seats within the House of Lords. This I believe can work towards the good of the Church and the nation. Governments have a bad conscience about the poor, the homeless, the old, the sick and ethnic groups. They are disturbed by protests against militarism, nuclear energy and the like. They are worried about order and law. What prevents significant action by most governments is the power of capitalist finance, debt and other economic pressure. Internationally, political, economic and military alliances exert their own pressures. Politicians who adopt the kind of concerns that cry out from the heart of the people would be removed from the political arena forthwith. However at the present moment Bishops cannot be voted out of office. They are therefore in a unique position to speak for the grassroots.

Many people feel that the House of Lords is a place of privilege. Many Bishops feel that too. There is, however, the rightful use of what 'is' to influence what 'could be'. Many of our Bishops are deeply conscious of the contradictions in our society – and in the Church for that matter. Once again Metz is salient here: 'The Church's criticism of the erosion of values in our society has to link up with the critique of social structures in society. Here also our Churches could function as a pioneering force for social transformations that are not yet politically acceptable in our country. . . In such a move forward, two forces would meet together – the critique of society presented by the Bishops and the intentions of a Basic Community Church gradually developed in our society.'[19]

Basic Christian or Ecclesial Communities are not about idealism. Nor are they about perfection or necessarily about 'a better way of being the Church'. They are about 'breakthrough'. They are about people first and things second. They are about meeting people's need to belong, love, feel good and have direction and purpose. Basic Communities promote interdependence and a God-ordained self-reliance. They reduce isolation and look to the well-being of others, because they are rooted in believing commitment to the gospel of Jesus Christ. They are about 'having life in all its fullness' (John 10:10) but also about 'bearing one another's burdens . . . thereby fulfilling the law of Christ' (Galatians 6:2 adapted). Basic Communities are about the encouragement and development of conversion through the enrichment of personal spiritual experience. They are about choosing to resist, from the grassroots, the structures that oppress, exploit and cause anxiety. Their very nature creates a tension but can that be worse than our present indifference? The task of the Church in nucleus is to 'construct with Christ the community of love'.

Notes

1. *The Emergent Church*, J B Metz: SCM, p. 82.
2. *The Sane Alternative*, James Robertson: James Robertson, p. 65.
3. Metz, *op. cit.*, p. 85.
4. *The Liberation of the Church*, David Clark: NACCCAN. A seminal work historically, sociologically and prophetically about the role, place and function of Basic Christian Communities.
5. Metz, *op. cit.*, p. 87.
6. Called to Conversion, Jim Wallis: Harper and Row.
7. Metz, *op. cit.*, p. 46.
8. *Op. cit.*, p. 89.
9. 'A New Way of Being the Church', Andrew Kirk: *Grassroots*, May/June 1983 (Volume 9, no. 3), p. 7.
10. Kirk, *op. cit.*, p. 6.
11. Metz, *op. cit.*, p. 92.
12. Kirk, *op. cit.*, p. 7.
13. Kirk, *op. cit.*, p. 6.
14. 'Faith in the City', Church House Publishing – 'An audit for the local Church' appendix A, p. 367 and a revision of this published in October 1986 incorporating a Faith Audit. See also 'Social analysis in the light of the Gospel' by Sean Healy and Brigid Reynolds: Fodens, pp. 72–79.
15. *Constructing Local Theologies*, *op. cit.*, p. 16.
16. *Op. cit.*, p. 18.
17. *Op. cit.*, p. 18. Schreiter has developed the question of the creating of local theologies, the role of the theologian, prophet and poet, and how such local theologians are rooted in Gospel, Church and Culture. This book is worth careful study.
18. *Op. cit.*, p. 18.
19. Metz, *op. cit.*, p. 91.

Chapter Twelve

The Church – Community of Hope

Hope is the foundation for constructing with Christ the civilisation of love. This book is written in hope, yet basis for hope is often hard to find. The evidence exists that cataclysm threatens. If we are spared nuclear holocaust, social disintegration in large areas of our western culture will escalate to a point where disorder, riot, violence and all manner of mayhem will be commonplace. Oppression and restriction will be the methods used by governments of both right and left to maintain – or regain – law and order. About this I am not optimistic or hopeful. As Paul Simon has put it, 'The signs of the prophets are written on the subway walls.' The graffiti of violence, anger, hatred and prejudice are to be seen everywhere. A materialistic society has outcast the poor, the unemployed, the coloured, old, tired and hungry.

To be hopeful in such a situation appears naive. We began by questioning the relevance of the Church, recognising with Newbiggin that 'Christians are not distinguishable as people who live by different commitments from their neighbours'.[1] Such a distinction, where it exists, is a fundamental sign of hope. To have commitments that are different will for the majority of us involve a paradigm shift in attitudes and behaviour. The making of choices and the exercising of will is fundamental to commitment. There has to be an act of faith among

us that things can be different. To have hope is to call for
Christian people to move from dependence, to interdependence, choosing to act together for the sake of others. Within
that choice lies the will to resist; learning to change; allowing
conversion to be a process by which our values, attitudes and
relationships are transformed. Our religion has to be depri-
vatised. 'I have decided,' said someone to me recently, 'I cannot
pray with you because, we hold different views on things.' How
sad! What a grip privatisation of faith has upon us. How much
better the principle 'that one bears the other even when it is
unpleasant and there is no agreement . . .'[2]

I believe the construction of Basic Christian Communities
within the mainstream churches provides a way of hope for this
generation. Such communities could be 'an advance herald of
something new'[3], resisting the impending cataclysm. For many
years now prophetic signs have been among us in the form
of different community life styles.[4] Most of these have been
intentional, that is they have risen as a result of a particular
calling or need. Community of Celebration was formed to
renew worship in the church; L'Arche grew to meet the needs
of the mentally handicapped in society; Corrymeela to be an
agent for reconciliation in the conflict in Ulster – and so on.
Others have been less obvious. Among such are groups Helder
Camara describes as 'Abrahamic'. These are formed from
people in all cultures and societies who 'by choice or necessity
throw in their lot together, abandon what is stable and secure,
and set out like pilgrims to see what God is really saying in
their concrete situations within our modern society.'[5] Such
groups are perceived as 'voices in the wilderness'. Many who
comprise the membership of such groups are Christians in local
or national government, politics, trade unions, charitable and
voluntary agencies. Perhaps because of that they have a
capacity for being prophetic, speaking out against an uncritical
acceptance of the status quo.

Abrahamic groups have a sense of 'anticipating the dream'
– working towards the establishment of communities where the

'love of God for the oppressed, the unloved, the unfree is characterised and revealed by God in Christ'. To make this possible, members commit themselves to a prophetic lifestyle. It is selfgiving; recognising that members exist not for themselves but for others. It is prophetic because it is shared in a spirit of renunciation, which is the basis for hope. Being prophetic means being free from the fear of failure and the need to succeed. It also means being free from self-rightousness and that carping judgement that freezes many a warm heart.

No group of people seeking to hear what God is really saying within the circumstances of today can be afraid of getting dirty hands. All kinds of pressures exist to conform to the values and intentions that surround us. 'Valuing integrity and truth more than loyalty to a political party or organisation'[6] is always the standard by which prophetic action and interaction must be judged. Recently I was sharing in a vigil on Hiroshima Day, when the person standing beside me, a leading Labour Party activist, said he had liked an article I had written on the Bomb. However he objected strongly to the stance that I had taken on abortion. I explained to him that as a Christian I could not be doctrinaire on different subjects, that my reasons for opposition to the Bomb were the same as my reasons for opposition to abortion. Being doctrinaire is anathema to being prophetic. Prophets get their hands dirty but keep their integrity. When God's people are faithful they sense his presence and joy in a way which the world simply cannot understand.

Conversion through contemplation

Renunciation and sacrifice are the fruits of contemplation. Activism rather than contemplation is the dominant expression of Christian practice in the West. Activism distracts us from what Thomas Merton describes as 'the curious state of alienation and confusion of man in modern society . . .' It distracts us from our own doubts, insecurity, sense of lostness, guilt and sin. Contemplation sounds mysterious, difficult even to

Western faith. Yet, at its simplest, it is learning, as Jesus did, to so reflect on God the Father, that our lifestyle, our social and political stances, all flow from that encounter.

Contemplation enables conversion. During my early Christian pilgrimage I attended many evangelistic-type rallies. I frequently felt the need to be 'converted' again. My perception of conversion then was that it was a cut-and-dried experience. One was at one moment not a Christian, and at another, by an act of will and repentance with faith, now a Christian. I do not want to be dismissive of this – it is part of who I am. The reason for mentioning it is simple. At those moments of personal spiritual crisis, I experienced an enormous sense of dread. I have since understood this as being integral to the ongoing process of conversion. It has been described like this: 'The deep root of. . . dread is the inner conflict which makes us guess that in order to be true to God and to ourselves, we must break with the familiar, established and secure norms and go off into the unknown. "Unless a man hates his father and mother . . . " These words of Christ give some indication of the deep conflict which underlies all Christian conversion in returning to a freedom based no longer on social approval and relative alienation, but on direct dependence on an invisible and inscrutable God, in pure faith.'[7]

It is knowing the cost of the choice to be made that is so awesome. Each of us faces doubt and self questioning, particularly when we have sought to understand the meaning of life. It is only when we allow solitude to enter our lives that we find how strong are the forces that oppose change within and around us. Prayer is 'yearning for the simple presence of God, for a personal understanding of his word, for the knowledge of his will and for capacity to hear and obey him. It is thus much more than uttering petitions for good things external to our deepest concerns.'[8]

Being who we are

Part of the process of knowing God is contemplating who we are. In giving himself the title '*I am*' in relation to his people, God revealed that his personhood is unique, known to him and knowable, at least in part, by others. There is within the rebelliousness of the human condition a desire to hide from God, and ourselves, the extent of that rebellion. Our capacity for self-deception is enormous. Yet with that self-deception, there is often self-denial. The denial of our true self is very often the process that prevents us from choosing to do God's will, and understanding how profoundly he is involved with the human condition.

There is about all of us a certain 'given-ness'. In our very creation within the womb there is a 'someone' to be known. Each is unique as a person with an identity that is truly 'God given'. Jeremiah understood this. 'Before I formed you within the womb I knew you; before you came to birth I consecrated you' (Jeremiah 1:4–5 JB). Consecration is understood here as meaning 'being full of potential'. In each person there is potential. How we develop is partly due to heredity and the environment in which we are brought up. Part of how our potential is used, depends on our willingness to allow significant change to take place within us, so that God can release the 'self' he perceived at conception. Jeremiah was told, 'I have appointed you (with all your potential – and given who you are) as a prophet to the nations' (Jeremiah 1:5, parentheses mine).

Contemplation is understood by many as the process by which inward peace is gained. That is true. But that is the end, rather than the beginning or the continuing of the process. To discover ourselves in the presence of God is frequently a disruptive process. We discover our inertia, our egoism, our self-deception. We recognise that so often we cry 'peace, peace, when there is no peace'. We convince ourselves that our lives, attitudes, political and social preferences are 'not too bad' – that we live 'good lives'.

If contemplative prayer is to bring us peace – it can only do so as we recognise that 'our "good lives" are . . . basically inauthentic, "good" only as long as they permit us to remain established in our respectable and impermeable identities. The "goodness" of such lives depends on the security afforded by relative wealth, recreation, spiritual comfort, and a solid reputation for piety. Such "goodness" is preserved by routine and the habitual avoidance of serious risk – indeed of serious challenge. In order to avoid apparent evil, this pseudo-goodness will ignore the summons of genuine good. It will prefer routine duty to courage and creativity. In the end it will be content with established procedures and safe formulas, while turning a blind eye to the greatest enormities of injustice and uncharity.'[9]

Abrahamic, that is pilgrim, communities have learned the true place of contemplation, renunciation and sacrifice; in so doing they have become prophetic. In being prophetic they have become free, to live at peace with God and those of goodwill. They have learned that self-giving not self-righteousness is the prerogative of the prophet. Such groups show us the potential for 'a new way of being the Church'.

Any such new way of being the Church will call for communities of people in every congregation to recognise that this is God's way of doing and being the Church. Through renunciation, sacrifice, contemplation, community and prophetic living God recreates the Church. This is the way we become distinguishable from our neighbours, living as advance heralds of hope.

The temptation of relevance

The hope of basic Christian communities is that they will be instruments for 'constructing with Christ the civilisation of love.' The heartbeat of the Church of the poor is love, and its ambition, the 'Kingdom on earth as it is in heaven'. A kingdom in which people can live in harmony and peace. A true civilisation. In establishing such a dream, that Church is experiencing what Jesus described: 'The kingdom of heaven has been subjected to violence and the violent are taking it by storm' (Matthew 11:12). The poor and the downcast are pushing the religious and the pious out of the way, in order to get into the Kingdom.

In the wilderness Jesus faced the temptation to be relevant. Each time he performed an act of healing, or demonstrated the nature of the rule of God through feeding the hungry, providing wine for a feast, or raising the dead he risked being misunderstood – seen simply as a wonder worker. The feeding of hungry people, the clothing of the naked, the sheltering of the homeless, are all commended by Jesus as things to be done. They are relevant and are appreciated. All God's people should have such matters as their concern. So why question the struggle to be relevant?

Much preaching and living of a gospel that has social and political concerns at its heart comes to grief at this point. The Christian gospel is distinctive. It is, as we have seen, the means by which humanity is liberated to become the people of God. Jesus made choices, spoke and acted, so that the authorities had very little choice but to execute him. Nevertheless they still crucified the Son of God. His death has the power to remove the guilt of a sinner, once that sin is acknowledged. To lose that perspective is to misrepresent the gospel. Jesus was faced with options – options that quickly became temptations. He had the choice to be relevant, spectacular and powerful (Matthew 4).

'To turn stones into bread' is such a reasonable option, that to reduce it to the level of a temptation seems positively scandalous. Yet Jesus' reply 'one does not live by bread alone but on every word that comes from the mouth of God' reveals a deeper truth. The importance of bread is relative. Jesus recalled the words of Moses who, in the face of grumblings of a hungry people, petitioned God for food in the desert. The people were fed with manna. Moses, aware of the significance of this provision, tells the people, 'God humbled you, he made you feel hunger, he fed you with manna which neither you nor your fathers had known, to make you understand that man does not live on bread alone, but that man lives on everything that comes from the mouth of God . . . from this. . . . your God was training you. . . Keep the commandments of the Lord your God, and so follow his ways and reverence him' (Deuteronomy 8:3–5).

Henri Nouwen puts it like this: 'Bread is given us by God so that we will trust ourselves completely to his word. Accomplishments, gifts and productivity are gifts given to those whose hearts are fixed on the Lord first. What this says is not that relevant behaviour should be despised, but that it should not be the basis of our identity as Christians.'[10]

It is important that we learn that 'we are not the bread we offer, but people who are fed by the Word of God and who find there true selfhood'.[11] As we risk taking God's word into ourselves and being nourished and reshaped by it, so we will grow into people who are free and fearless, witnessing that God is present and active in his world. Sometimes we will have to bear the accusation of irrelevance. That is the time when we most need to hold on to the conviction that neither success or failure are our measure. Faithfulness to God's word and faith in him give our lives relevance. Lest we get pious about this, we ought to recognise that temptations to be relevant, powerful or spectacular are life-long temptations. They are especially invidious in a culture like ours because they are so much a part of the way we have been nurtured and educated. Our lives are geared to success, achievement, meaning and influence. We live in an 'upwardly socially mobile environment' – acceptance in our society means getting more and having more, by being better than others.

The way up is down

The heart of God's activity in Christ – the incarnation – is the very antithesis of an upward social mobility. God comes down to us in Christ. It is a downward social mobility. His process is downward: child, servant, slave, victim. He comes to the sinful and the sinned against. He becomes subject to the powerful by being powerless. He enters his glory by suffering (Luke 24.26) and his greatness by slavery (Matthew 20:26–28). If we want his way it is the way of the cross – and the path is downward. 'Anyone who does not take his cross and follow me is not worthy of me. Anyone who finds his life will lose it; anyone who loses his life for my sake will find it' (Matthew 10:39).

'Somewhere deep in our heart we already know that success, fame, influence, power and money do not give us inner joy and peace for which we crave. Somewhere we can even sense a certain envy of those who have shed all their ambitions and live their lives in simple obedience. Yes, somewhere we can even get a taste of that mysterious joy in the smile of those who have nothing to lose.'[12]

The hope of God in Christ is that the incarnation will become visible day by day in his people. Jesus was not a rugged individualist, he lived in a community. His disciples and the women who travelled with him were an itinerant community. They practised what they preached. They were often without shelter – 'The Son of man has nowhere to lay his head' (Luke 9:58).

They depended for hospitality on the goodwill of those who had homes. On their mission travels they looked for those who would receive them into their homes. They learnt to 'shake dust off their feet' against those who refused to offer hospitality and hear the Good News.

A Community of sinners

As a community they were quarrelsome, disloyal, disobedient and protective. They found it hard to understand the true nature of Jesus' objectives, and could see no sense in the choices he made. While being their leader, he embarrassed them by his approach – washing feet after tiresome journeys, taking notice of children, women, tax collectors and blind beggars. They were jealous, competitive, critical, frequently frightened and often deeply confused. For whole stretches of time Jesus would wander off, reappearing in circumstances that were frequently awkward and even dangerous. They had to do a lot for themselves – and when Jesus did do something for them, they always had to learn some lesson from it. On one such occasion, in spite of much human effort the disciples were unable to heal a boy with a deaf and dumb spirit. As a community they were frequently broke and often unable to pay their rightful dues, to the extent that on one occasion the most unconventional fund-raising is entered upon (Matthew 17:24–27.). In spite of this Jesus allowed people to be reckless and irresponsible from time to time, notably when a woman poured an expensive jar of scent all over him!

Yet, it was that mutuality, that sense of belonging, that gave them the training and discipline to become such an extra-ordinary movement for change. They learnt to bear with one another, to pray, and to give others an opportunity to be used in the service of God and their fellow human beings. Within such a framework they learnt the value of shared resources, and discovered how to use and recognise gifts that lay dormant among them. Above all, they learnt the true cost of service and that the true goal is freedom.

The community that surrounded Jesus during his ministry learned of a leadership that did not express itself in status terms. Jesus brought people together and shared with them his values and concerns. Jesus facilitated the disciples to become leaders in their own right. He bonded people together – how else could the primitive community in the Acts have emerged so unscathed by events? By his freedom, he freed others to make changes within their own lifestyle, in their ways of doing and being.

During the 1930's Dietrich Bonhoeffer formed a community at Finkenwald in Germany – the nucleus of the 'Confessing Church'. This church, perceiving the ambitions and intentions of a nation state bent on genocide, sought to find within itself the resolve and inner conviction to confront that state in the name and power of Jesus Christ. The community lived and worked under a simple rule, which is outlined in Bonhoeffer's book *Life Together*.[13] Bonhoeffer recognised that 'if you love peace, then hate injustice, hate tyranny, hate greed – but hate these things in yourself and not another'.[14] In describing how the community worshipped, prayed together, served together he observed: 'Christians often remain isolated; the final break through to real fellowship is not achieved because they form a fellowship of believers, as devout Christians, but not as irreligious people, as sinners. Consequently each must conceal his sins from himself and the community. . . It is in confession that the break through occurs. Sin seeks to be alone with the person involved, it draws him away from the community. . . In confession the light of the Gospel breaks into the darkness and stubbornness of the heart.'[15] Hope for true fellowship among God's people comes when the common sinfulness of all is seen. No civilisation of God's love is possible without that recognition.

Community grows from compassion

Basic Christian community must be formed from within a spirituality that acknowledges hope as its foundation. That hope is Christ, whose kingdom of love and justice can be revealed. Such a spirituality calls for conversion, contemplation, renunciation, sacrifice and fellowship rooted in the milieu of downward social mobility, prayer, resistance, community, and confession of our common humanity.

While seeking to be rooted biblically and within the context of scriptural understanding, building basic Christian communities is not about trying to 'recreate' that which existed uniquely in the primitive church (Acts 2; Acts 4). Neither is it about trying to translate a model from Latin America directly into our own situation. It is not about being cosy, secure, even nostalgic. 'Nostalgia for an idealised past does not contain the seeds of new life.'[16] There are no blue prints for building basic communities. This book has deliberately resisted trying to lay out blueprints on 'how to form a Basic Christian Community'. Among some it will be criticised for that. Communities, however, grow and occur. They begin when people sense their isolation, their loneliness, fear and powerlessness. Community develops around people who share a common desire to care for the other, or as a response to the pain of a particular locality. 'Where true Christian Community is formed compassion happens in the world. . .'[17] When people gather together in Christ's name and take on his yoke in humbleness and gentleness of heart (Matthew 11:29.), wherever men and women let go of their old anxious ways of thinking and find each other in the mind of Christ, then community happens.

Community must happen in the Church. However inadequate, frustrating and compromised we may appear – 'We are the Body of Christ.' If we hate the church, we hate the Body, and in some measure at least we hate the Head – Jesus Christ our Lord. We must repent of our hatred. We must look upon his fractured Body as one that is a sign for the healing of the nations.

Basic communities can provide new life for the established and institutional Church. They need not threaten its historicity and authority. Without the development of such groups we shall be assigned to a future of middle class conservative religion in the suburbs and other places of prosperity. In the inner cities and urban priority areas of our land Christian witness will continue to decline, despite the best efforts of hard pressed clerics and others to halt it. Basic Christian Communities could liberate the Church to work effectively in the soulless areas of the inner city and urban developments. Middle-class Christians in communities would be free to work with them on the margins. The Basic Christian Community in Latin America has been described as 'leaven and first fruit of an ecclesial model that is communitarian, prophetic and liberating'. Could that happen here? I hope so!

Notes

1. 'Mission in the 1980's', *op cit*.
2. *The Open Church*, Jurgen Moltmann: SCM, p. 33.
3. J B Metz, *op. cit.*
4. See David Clark's *Liberation of the Church* (NACCCAN) for a comprehensive study of these.
5. 'The Church as agent for social change', Thomas Cullinson, *Doing Theology in a Divided World*, p. 137.
6. *Op. cit.*, p. 137.
7. *Contemplative Prayer*, Thomas Merton: Darton Longman & Todd, pp. 26, 27
8. *Op. cit.*, pp. 82, 83.
9. *Op. cit.*, p. 130.
10. 'Temptation', Henri Nouwen: *Sojourners*, July 1981.
11. *Op. cit.*, p. 26.
12. 'The Selfless Christ', Henri Nouwen: *Sojourners*, June 1981.
13. *Life Together*, Dietrich Bonhoeffer: SCM.
14. *Seeds of Contemplation*, Thomas Merton.
15. *Households of God*, David Parry: Darton Longman & Todd, p. 182 (quoted by author).
16. *Op. cit.*, p. 73.
17. *Compassion, op. cit.*, p. 57.